一力文库 018

道德箴言录

[法]拉罗什福科 著
王 水 译

上海三联书店

图书在版编目（CIP）数据

道德箴言录／〔法〕拉罗什福科著；王水译．－上海：
上海三联书店，2008.7
（一力文丛）
ISBN 978-7-5426-2776-6

Ⅰ．道… Ⅱ．①拉…②王… Ⅲ．道德修养－箴言－汇编－法国 Ⅳ．B825

中国版本图书馆 CIP 数据核字（2008）第 085034 号

道德箴言录

著　　者／〔法〕拉罗什福科
译　　者／王　水
责任编辑／戴　俊　　叶　庆
装帧设计／张岩宏
监　　制／研　发
出版发行／上海三联书店

　　（200031）中国上海市乌鲁木齐南路 396 弄 10 号
　　　　　http://www.sanlianc.com
　　　　　E-mail:shsanlian@yahoo.com.cn

印　　刷／北京凯达印务有限公司
版　　次／2008 年 7 月第 1 版
印　　次／2008 年 7 月第 1 次印刷
开　　本／640×965　1/16
字　　数／56 千字
印　　张／6.75

ISBN 978-7-5426-2776-6/G · 909
定　价：20.50 元

1

人们所称之德行，往往不过是大量的、种类各异的行为和利害关系，由天赋机遇或者后天勤奋精妙构成。男人成为勇士并不都是因为英勇，女人成为贞女也并不都是因为贞洁。

2

自爱乃是至上的自我奉承。

3

无论人们已在自爱之领域发现了什么，那个领域仍有人类未曾勘察之未知。

4

自爱之精明，甚于世上最精明之人。

5

人们的激情存续之期，不会长于生命中断之时。

6

激情常使最聪明之人变得愚蠢，有时又可使最愚蠢之人变得聪明。

7

那些令人眼花缭乱的伟大而卓越的行动，在政治家们强烈的图谋下表现出来；而不是表现为性格和激情的结果。因此，奥古斯都与安东尼的斗争——那战争被视为是他们心怀主宰世界的野心而引发，也许那仅仅是嫉妒的结果。

8

激情是唯一始终都在进行说服工作的鼓动家。激情乃人之天生技艺，其规则是认为自己永远正确无误；头脑最简单的人一旦拥有激情，其劝诱能力将会远胜于虽最能雄辩但却激情寡淡之人。

9

激情多有不公义，抑或过于自我，可致使其跟随者陷入险境；实践中，我们对他的信任应需谨慎，即便是它们表现得最富可信度。

10

人们内心深处源源不断地产生激情，故此，一种激情的破灭几乎总是意味着另一种激情的产生。

11

激情常常走向自己的反面：吝啬有时导致挥霍，挥霍有时导致吝啬；我们常常经由软弱而达到坚强，经由怯懦而达到勇敢。

12

无论人们如何煞费苦心把激情隐藏于虔诚和光荣的外衣下，激情总会透过其遮蔽物而昭然显现。

13

人们的自爱所难以忍受的谴责，来自趣味的更甚于来自判断力的。

14

人们不仅无视利害，还会恩将仇报，忘记屈辱。连必要的复仇或报恩，似乎也成了他们不愿意承受的苦役。

15

君主的仁慈往往只是笼络民心的手段。

16

被人们视为可产生美德的仁慈，其动机有时是虚荣，有时是懒惰，有时是恐惧，但几乎所有的时候又是三者的合一。

17

幸福之人的节制来源于好运气赋予他们性情的镇定宁静。

18

节制产生之因，不过是害怕遭受他人的嫉妒和轻蔑而已，节制这种美德总降临到那些正陶醉于自身好运的人们身上。节制是人们精神力量的一次愚蠢自负的展示——简言之，人们节制的制高点在于意图证实自身比命运之安排还要强大。

19

我们每个人都有足够的力量去促成他人的不幸。

20

智者的坚定不移，仅仅是他们用以隐藏内心躁动的艺术。

21

那些被判死罪的人们，有时会对死亡做出坚定不移或者傲视的姿态，这其实恰恰是害怕面对死亡；所以，人们可以说，这种坚定不移和傲视的态度于他们的精神，就像蒙住眼睛的绷带于他们的眼睛。

22

哲学能轻易地战胜昔日之痛和未来之痛，然而，却在今日之痛前败下阵来。

23

几乎无人能认识死亡，人们只能承受它。通常出于决心，甚至是出于愚钝和惯性来承受它，许多人死去是因为他们把死亡看作不得不接受的事实。

24

当那些大人物被持续不断的厄运击垮时，人们才发现他们过去只是靠野心而不是智慧支撑自己；承担着巨大的自负虚荣，英雄们所行所为与常人无异。

25

承担好运所需的德行，要多于承担厄运所需的德行。

26

直视太阳和死亡，不能不眨眼。

27

人们常常以他们的激情为荣，即使是最糟糕的激情；但嫉妒却是一种既羞怯又谦逊的激情，以至没有人敢承认拥有它。

28

猜忌在某种意义上尚有公正合理性，因为它倾向于使人们保护属于自己或认为是属于自己的利益。相反，妒忌却是一种狂怒，使人们无法忍受别人的幸运。

29

人们的善良品性，往往比人们所行之恶更能招致迫害和憎恨。

30

我们所拥有的力量超过我们所拥有的意愿,我们经常仅仅为了找借口申辩而说某些事是不可能的。

31

如果我们自己完美无瑕,就不会从注意他人的缺点中获得那么多的乐趣。

32

猜忌生长于疑惑之中,当人们经由疑惑直至确定无疑时,猜忌要么立即消除,要么演变成一种狂怒。

33

骄傲总能自我弥补,什么也不会遗失,即使在它抛弃空虚的时候。

34

如果我们自己不怀骄傲之心,我们就不会怨恨他人之骄傲。

35

所有人的骄傲乃是一致的,唯一的不同在于其表现方法和手段各异。

36
正像自然非常精致地安排了我们身体的各种器官，以使我们能感悟幸福，它也给我们安排了骄傲，以使我们感觉不到自身不理性之耻。

37
在我们埋怨那些有缺点的人们时，骄傲是比善行更有效的方法，我们与其责备他们改正错误，不如让他们明白：我们可没有他们那些缺点毛病。

38
人们因满怀希望而许诺，因心存敬畏而履约。

39
利益用各式各样的语言说话，表现出各式各样的特征；甚至出自无私的利益也是如此。

40
利益使一些人盲目，使另一些人眼明。

41

那些太专注琐碎小事的人，往往对大事不堪胜任。

42

人们没有足够的力量和勇气以完全追随理智。

43

当一个人被他人所引导时，他往往认为是自己在引导自己；而当他凭自己心智朝某个确定目标努力时，他的精神不知不觉将他引向另一个目标。

44

精神强盛或精神脆弱，其实命名不当，他们实际上不过是人们身体器官的优良或知足而已。

45

人们情绪的反复无常，比运气的反复无常还要奇怪和不可理喻。

46

哲学家们对生命表现出的眷恋或冷淡，只不过是他们自爱的口味不同，对此我们无需做过多争论，就像不必争论人们对腭间味觉或者某一色调的偏好。

47
我们的情绪为命运赠予我们的每件礼物都确定出价格。

48
幸福得之于体验，而非事物本身所系。人们因得到自己的所爱而幸福，不会因得到他人的爱之物而幸福。

49
我们从未像我们想象的那样幸福，也从未像我们想象的那样不幸。

50
那些自视有德行的人使自己相信荣耀来自不幸，并使他人和他们自己都相信这一点：成为命运的靶子是有价值和可敬的。

51
再没有什么能如此消减我们的自满之心了——

我们看到，在某一时刻我们极力赞成的东西，在另一个时刻我们却又极力反对。

52

无论人们的命运表现得有多悬殊，然而世间仍然存有某种可使好运与厄运相互均衡的补偿。

53

无论天赋如何有优势，仅有这些远远不够，造就英雄还需要时势运气。

54

哲学家们对财富的蔑视，不过是一种深藏的对不公正命运的报复心理。这种蔑视是护佑他们不致跌落于贫困中的秘诀，通过这种路径相反的方法，他们取得了依靠财富不可能得到的显赫声望。

55

对恩惠的厌恶不过是爱好恩惠的另一种方式。没有蒙恩的人，对蒙恩者表示出嫉妒，可安慰和缓解自己没有得到的恩惠的苦恼；如果不能夺走那些人用以吸引世人注意的东西，人们就拒绝给他们以尊敬。

56
为了在世间获取成功，人们首先竭力表现出已经取得世间成功的样子。

57
尽管人们因自己的伟大业绩而高兴，但他们更多只是机遇的产物，而非一个伟大谋划的结果。

58
人们的行动看似充满了幸运或不幸，人们对这些行动的大量褒贬就取决于这些幸运或不幸。

59
再不幸的事件，精明之人也能从中汲取有益的东西；再幸运的事件，愚蠢之人也能把它弄得对己有害。

60
命运女神会扭转一切事件，以使她青睐之人获益。

61

人们的幸福或不幸依赖于他们性格的程度，不亚于依赖他们运气的程度。

62

真诚乃是心灵不设防的敞开；我们只能在极少数人身上找到它；我们日常所见的真诚，不过是一种为了赢得他人信任而做出的狡猾伪饰。

63

厌恶谎言，常常出于一种不易觉察的野心，是想使我们的话语更具可信度和影响力，并想给我们的会话赋予虔诚严谨的外表。

64

真理在世间所行之善，并没有假冒它的伪真理所行之恶那么多。

65

人们把赞美慷慨地加在"审慎"之上，但它在最小的事情上也不能确保我们平安无虞。

66

聪明人必须管控好他的利益的次序，使之井然有序。因为我们的贪欲时常困扰我们，使我们在同一时间内追逐太多的利益，结果，我们过于热切地寻求最小利益之时，我们恰恰痛失获取最大利益之机。

67

优雅之于身体，犹如良知之于精神。

68

对爱下定义是很困难的，我们只能说：在灵魂层面，爱是一种统治欲；在精神层面，爱是一种同情心；在身体层面，它则是一种潜藏的、精巧的愿望，意图占有那赋加了神秘色彩的我们所钟爱的事物。

69

如果存在一种纯粹的爱，它不曾与我们其他的激情相掺杂混合，那么，这种爱是潜藏在心灵最深处的爱，甚至连我们自身都觉察不到它的存在。

70

爱情所至之处，不能长期躲在伪装下；爱情未至之处，亦不能长期伪装其存在。

71

当人们的爱情不再持续时，几乎都会为自己曾有过的爱情而羞耻。

72

如果我们根据爱的主要效果来判断，爱情更像是恨而不是爱。

73

我们可以发现那些从未放纵于私情之中的女子，却极鲜见有过放纵却仅仅一次的女子。

74

爱情只有一种，但其副本却有千差万别的面孔。

75

爱情和火焰，非得永恒不断地更新，否则就难以存续；爱情和火焰，一旦停止希望或停止畏惧，它们的生命活力就会停止。

76
真正的爱情就像真正的幽灵那样飘忽不定：所有人都在谈论它，但却没有几人亲眼见过它。

77
爱情把它的名字借给无以计数的商业式婚约及交往，然而，爱情和那些有着它特征的事件之间的关系，少之又少，简直就像共和国总督和发生在威尼斯的那些事的关系。

78
大多数人热爱正义，不过是因为他们害怕遭受不公正。

79
对缺乏自信者而言，沉默乃其处事时的最佳良策。

80
我们交友如此多变，是因为我们难以认识灵魂的本性，却容易看到智力的优点。

81

除了那符合我们心意的事物外，我们什么也不爱。当我们爱朋友甚于爱自己时，那也不过是遵循自己的趣味和喜好而已。然而，正是靠这种唯一的爱朋友胜过爱自己的情意，友谊才可能是真实和完美的。

82

与敌人的和解，只是出于一种想改善自己境况的欲望，出于对战争的厌倦，对一些意外不幸事件的敬畏。

83

人们定义为"友爱"的，其实质不过是一种社会交往关系，一种对各自利益的尊重和相互间的协作。事实上，它只不过是一种交易，自爱总是期盼能从这种交易里赚取某些东西。

84

不信任自己的朋友比被朋友欺骗更为可耻。

85

我们经常自以为我们爱某些人胜过爱我们自己，然而，仅仅是利益才是形成人们友谊的，我们将自己的友谊给别人，并非是出于我们的行善之心，而是为了有朝一日能得到他们的回报。

86

人们的提防之心，证实了别人的欺骗。

87

如果人们彼此之间没有尔虞我诈、相互欺骗，人们就不可能在社会中长久生存。

88

人们根据自爱对朋友的满意程度，在心目中扩大或者削减朋友们的优点，人们按照别人向自己展示出的生活方式来判断他们的美德与价值。

89

人人都为自己的记忆力引以为憾，从来没有人抱怨自己的判断力。

90

在生活交往中，人们更经常地是由于我们的缺点而不是由于我们的优点而喜欢我们的。

91

在通向目标的道路上遇到不可能逾越的障碍时，最执著强大的野心会表现得微乎其微。

92

要使一个人从自高自大中醒悟过来，就得向对待那个雅典疯子那样对待他，那个雅典疯子洋洋自得地认为世间所有港口的船只，都归他所有。

93

老年人因能给人以良好的教诲而欣慰，其实是因为他们再也不能把自己树立成坏典型了。

94

伟大的称号对那些不知如何维系它的人们来说，只会使他们退步而非振奋。

95

卓越出众的功勋有这样一个明显标志:那些嫉妒它的人,也不得不赞美它。

96

一个人也许是忘恩负义的,但往往,他在忘恩负义方面的过错,并不比那个施予他好处的人多。

97

如果我们认为理智和洞察力是两个完全不同的东西,那么,我们就被它们蒙骗了。洞察力只是理智之光的扩展,理智之穿透到事物深处,并在那里注意值得注意的一切,在那里觉察似乎不可觉察之物。因此,我们必须承认:那些被我们归之于产生自洞察力的所有效果,也属于理智之光的范围。

98

每个人都赞美自己心灵美好,但没有人有胆量如此赞美自己的理解力。

99

精神的高雅在于思索有道德的思想和凝练精确

的思想。

100

精神的勇敢就是以一种令人惬意的方式谈论那些最为空洞的事物。

101

想法总是在我们的头脑中一闪而过,在我们能捕捉并雕琢它们之前完美地呈现出来。

102

精神总是心灵的受骗者。

103

那些能够认识到自己精神的人,未必都能认识到自己的心灵。

104

各种人和事物都有自己的观察点,对人及事物作出正确判断,有的时候需要近距离去观察,有的时候却恰恰相反,需要站在远处方可准确判断。

105

那些能偶然发觉理性的人并不是有理性的,能认识、辨别、检验理性的人才是有理性的。

106

为了正确地了解事物,我们应当了解其中的细枝末节,由于事物的细枝末节是无穷无尽的,我们的知识也就始终是肤浅且有缺憾的。

107

以自己从不卖弄风情而自吹自擂,这本身即是一种卖弄。

108

精神难以长时期地扮演心灵的角色。

109

青年人根据血液的热度而改变自己的趣味,老年人则根据习惯而保持自己的趣味。

110

没有任何东西能像"建议"那样被我们如此慷慨地送出。

111

我们爱一个女人越多,就越倾向于憎恨她。

112

精神上的瑕疵和脸上的瑕疵一样,因年龄而增加。

113

存在一种婚姻,它美好但却无快乐可言。

114

当我们被敌人所欺骗或者被友人所出卖时,我们伤心不已;但当这欺骗和出卖来自我们自己时,我却往往会心甘情愿。

115

欺骗自己和欺骗他人一样容易。

116

再没有什么事情比寻求劝告或给予劝告更不真诚的事了：寻求劝告者会对他朋友的意见表现出一副顺从尊重的样子，然而他内心所希望的却是让他的朋友赞同他的意见，并为他的意见所导致的后果承担一定的责任；而那给予劝告者，则表现出一副真挚热情的无私模样来回报朋友的信任，然而他在给朋友提出劝告时，通常是以自己的私利或自己的名誉为导向的。

117

我们所有行为中最为狡猾的是，假装自己没有看到别人为我们设置的圈套，因为人们在打算欺骗别人之时，往往是自己最容易受骗之时。

118

心中从不存在欺瞒他人的念头，往往会导致更容易地受到他人欺骗。

119

我们太习惯于向别人伪装自己，以至最后我们向自己伪装自己。

120

人们的背叛行为更多地是出于软弱，而不是出于某种既定的背叛动机。

121

我们行善的目的，常常是为了能够不受惩罚地作恶。

122

如果我们战胜了激情的诱惑，这更多因为激情自身的脆弱易逝而非是我们意志的坚定刚强。

123

如果我们不自我奉承，我们大概也能拥有快乐，但那也必是微乎其微的。

124

最富欺诈性的人，会毕其一生谴责欺骗，他们这样做的目的，是为了在某个关键场合，自己行使欺骗之术，以为自己谋取更大的利益。

125

经常使用阴谋诡计，意味着此人拥有一颗智力有限的头脑，一般而言，那些使用诡计的人在某一方面把自己受到尊重的保护，但在另一方面却让自己暴露在他人抨击之中。

126

阴谋诡计和背信弃义，都是无能的产物。

127

上当受骗的最可靠途径，就是认为自己比别人更精明。

128

聪明过度是一种欺骗性的明智，真正的明智乃是一种稳重的聪明。

129

为避免被奸诈之人所骗，有些时候做些傻事是必要的。

130

软弱是人们唯一不会改正的缺点。

131

对那些拿爱情当饭吃的女人来说,制造爱情不过是她们所有缺点中最小的那个缺点。

132

对待别人客观明智,总会比对待自己客观明智,更方便易行。

133

世间最完美的模型,可以使我们通过它,看出原形本身的缺陷和荒谬。

134

我们表现得最为荒谬可笑时,不是因为我们具有某些品性习惯,更多的原因是我们假装具有某些品性习惯。

135

有时我们会同自己不一致,这种不一致甚至比我们与他人的差异还要大。

136

有一些人如果不是听人谈及爱情，他们根本就不会去爱。

137

当没有虚荣心作祟时，我们无话可说。

138

我们更喜欢谈论自己的不幸，而不是说那些无关紧要之事。

139

在交谈中使我们发现极少有通情达理和令人愉快的人，一个原因是：几乎没有人不是更多地关注自己想说的，而不是如何能确切回答人们对他说的。那些最机灵聪明和礼貌周至的人，也充其量只是向他人作出一副正在倾听的样子。与此同时，我们可以从他们的精神和眼睛中，感知到一种对我们所说的话茫然不解的神色，和一种急于将谈话内容引到他们关心的话题上去的意图。他们并没有这样想：

那样力求使自己惬意是一个取悦或说服别人的坏办法，并且，好好地倾听，好好地回复是我们在谈话中所能拥有的最大的魅力之一。

140

如果没有愚蠢之人相伴，幽默风趣之人常常会陷入困境，施展不开本领。

141

我们常常夸口说自己从不使人烦，我们因过分自负而觉察不到自己有多么的烦扰他人。

142

正如伟大精神的特征是平凡话语蕴含大道理，肤浅精神的特征则是滔滔不绝但空洞无力。

143

我们过分盛赞他人的优秀品质，与其说是出于对他们美德的尊重，不如说是出于对我们自己意见的尊重。我们想吸引到他人的赞美，似乎是我们造就了他们。

144

我们并非喜好赞美他人,如果没有动力我们决不赞美任何人。赞美是一种狡猾、隐秘和精巧的奉承,它能给予赞美者和被赞美者不同的满足。得到赞美的人就仿佛那是对他美德的一个应有回报,送出赞美的人则是为了让自己的公正和辨别力引起他人注意。

145

我们经常选择的是某些有害于被赞美者的赞美,这可以从我们赞美人们的缺陷引起的反响中见到,这些缺陷是我们不敢以另一种方式揭示的。

146

通常,我们仅仅是为了得到赞美而赞美他人。

147

很少有人明智到这一程度:喜欢逆耳忠言,甚于喜欢顺耳佞语。

148

有一些责难其实是赞美,有一些赞美其实是责难。

149

拒绝他人赞美，不过是希望再次被赞美。

150

那种激励我们获取他人赞美的欲望，增强了我们的德行；我们给予理智、价值和美的赞美，也有助于增强我们的德行。

151

自己去统治他人容易，防止自己受他人统治很难。

152

如果我们没有自我奉承，别人的奉承就不会损害到我们。

153

天生本性产生美德，机遇运气成就业绩。

154

人们身上有些缺点毛病，运气能够改正，理智却改正不了。

155

有些人虽有才能却只招人厌恶，有些人虽有缺点过错却讨人喜欢。

156

有些人仅有的那些价值，在于在正确的时间内说些愚蠢的话、做些同样愚蠢的事，一旦他们改变了他们的行为，那会导致他们毁掉一切。

157

对那些负有盛名的大人物，应该用他们攫取荣誉的方法来评估他们的荣誉。

158

奉承是一枚伪币，只有我们的虚荣心使它有机会流通。

159

仅仅拥有崇高品性还远远不够，我们还应对其加以运用。

160

一项光辉伟大的行动，如果不是出于一个崇高伟大的动机，那也不应该受到人们的景仰和尊重。

161

如果我们期望从行为与思想导致的所有后果中做出评价的话，在行为和思想之间应当存在某种确定的和谐状态。

162

对自己平庸资质巧妙规划利用以赢得荣誉，往往能比那些真正出众的人赢得更多的尊敬和名声。

163

无数行为表现得愚蠢鲁莽，其背后潜藏的动机却是十分明智慎重。

164

显出一副配得上自己没有得到的职位的模样，要比胜任自己正在从事的工作更为容易。

165

真正公道者对他人的真正价值予以尊敬，普通大众却将他人的真正价值视为幸运。

166

世界往往对功绩的外表而非功绩本身予以报酬奖赏。

167

相比慷慨大方，吝啬贪婪更与节俭理财相背离。

168

尽管"希望"富有欺骗性，但她引领我们在愉悦惬意中，走向生命的终点。

169

明明是懒惰闲散和怯懦敬畏使我们不得不行进在履行义务的道路上，但我们的德行却因之不断受到世人赞美褒扬。

170

即使一项行动表现出正当而忠诚，仍很难判断它的动机是出于正直还是耍花招。

171

德行消失在自我利益之中，正如江河消失在海洋之中。

172

如果彻底深入地研究一下冷漠的各种影响，我们会发现它更多地是想摆脱责任而非舍弃利益。

173

有各种不同的求知欲：一种是出于利益——即想学会可能对我们有用的东西；另一种是出于骄傲——即想知道其他人不知道的东西。

174

运用理智最恰当的方式是：相对承受那些我们所能预料的即将到来的苦难，更理智的是能够承受那些已经降临的不幸和苦难。

175

爱情的坚贞不渝实际是一种永恒的反复无常，

这种反复无常使我们的感情接连不断地依附于我们的爱人的各种品质之上，时而给其中一个以偏爱，时而又偏爱另一个。因此，这种坚贞不渝不过是发生在同一对象身上的一种止而复行的无常。

176

有两种类型的坚贞不渝存在于爱情中：一种类型起因于人们能不断地在爱人那里发现值得去爱的新鲜点，另一种类型的忠贞不过由于人们把坚贞不渝视为可带来好名声的事物而坚持下来。

177

坚定不移并不值得特别谴责，也不值得特别赞美，因为它只不过是某些趣味和情感的持续，这些趣味和情感是我们既不能自我制作又不能自我给予的。

178

我们热爱学习新东西的原因，并不是我们对旧有知识的厌倦或对知识更新的渴望，而是因为厌倦了来自那些了解我们的人的有限的钦佩，因为我们渴望那些不太了解我们的人的更多的赞美。

179

有时我们会抱怨朋友们的轻率,以预先为自己开释。

180

我们的懊悔之心,是对我们已做过的错事满怀悲哀,更是对有可能降临到我们身上的后果感到的恐惧。

181

有一种变化无常,其根源是精神的轻率或软弱,它可使得我们接纳所有其他人的意见;另一种变化无常是言之有理、较可原谅的,因为它的根源是耽于物欲。

182

正如毒药进入了药物的范围那样,恶行也进入了德行的结构之中,审慎的聚集和混和它们,恶行和毒药也可用于抵抗人们生活中的诸多病端。

183

我们必须承认——这是使德性光荣的:人们的

最大不幸乃是被罪行所压倒的不幸。

184

我们承认自己的过错，是想用自己表现出的真诚来修复别人因我们的这些过错而对我们形成的不良评价。

185

世间既有邪恶之枭雄，亦有善良之英雄。

186

我们并不蔑视所有曾有过恶行之人，但我们蔑视所有毫无德行之人。

187

德行之名，和恶行之名，在我们谋取利益时同样有用。

188

灵魂的健康并不比身体的健康更有保障，当激情看似远远离开我们时，我们仍有被激情感染的危险，这危险程度并不亚于身体健康时会突然陷入疾病状态。

189

人们的天性似乎在每个人出生之时,就确定出了此人的善行和恶行的界限。

190

伟大卓绝之人,不应犯下滔天大错。

191

可以说,恶行等待在我们的人生必经之路上,就像旅店老板在路边等待不断到他那里临时借宿的行人那样,并且,即使我们获准在同一条路上再走一次,我仍怀疑我们那些所谓的经验教训是否真能使我们避开那些恶行。

192

当恶行主动离弃我们时,我们认为是自己遗弃了恶行,并就此自我奉承、自吹自擂。

193

灵魂的病端就像肢体的病端那样,总有故态萌发之时刻,我们所谓的"痊愈",往往不过是疾病的间断,抑或是不同疾病之间的转化。

194

灵魂的瑕疵恰如肢体的创伤,我们想尽一切办法去愈合它,但它的疤痕总是抹不平,那一道道伤口始终处于再次发作的危险之中。

195

人们之所以能预防沉溺于某一种恶行,其原因是人们身上还有太多其他的恶行。

196

当我们的缺点仅仅为我们自己所知时,我们很容易忽略它们的存在。

197

世上有这样一种人,如果不是我们亲眼看到他们的恶行,我们根本不会相信他们会作恶,然而,这其中只有极少数的行恶之人,值得人们为其行为大惊小怪、匪夷所思。

198

我们过分夸大渲染某些人的荣誉，是为了贬低另一些人的荣誉；并且，如果我们不想直接责备孔代亲王殿下和德雷纳元帅，我们只需减少对他们的溢美之辞即可。

199

那种想表现得精明的欲望，事实上却常常阻止人们真正变得精明。

200

如果没有虚荣心一路护送，德行走不了那么远。

201

如果有人认为，他能够脱离于整个世界而自足，是自欺欺人；但有人若认为人们不能在世界上保持独立，那就更是自欺欺人了。

202

假装诚实的人是那些在别人和自己面前遮掩自身缺陷的人；真正诚实的人是那些能够认识到自身

缺陷，并完全坦白和承认它们的人。

203
真正慎虑之人，决不会在任何事物中行激怒之举。

204
女人的冷漠是她们加诸于自身美貌之上的平衡木和担子。

205
女人的德行往往是她们对良好名声和宁静安逸之喜爱。

206
那些总想使自己置身于正派人视线监督之内的人，才是真正的正派人。

207
在我们一生中的各个阶段，愚蠢与我们如影随形；如果有谁表现出明智，那不过是因为他的愚蠢和他的年龄、运气相称而已。

208

有一些愚蠢之人，其自知之明在于知道如何巧妙地运用他们的傻劲。

209

生活中没有经历愚蠢，并不意味着活得如自己想象的那般明智。

210

在一天天变老的过程中，我们越来越愚蠢，也越来越明智。

211

有些人就像戏剧，我们只是在某个特定的时刻为它们送上赞美之辞。

212

大多数人判断他人的标准，仅仅是成功或者财富。

213

热爱荣誉、害怕耻辱、贪恋财富、奢求生活安逸舒适、妄图贬抑他人，这些都是促使人群中涌出勇敢者的原因。

214

在普通的战士们那里，勇敢是一种为了谋生而采用的危险方法。

215

完全的勇敢和完全的怯懦，都是极少见的两个极端。这两个极端间的空间很广大，可以容纳几乎所有类型的勇气，其差别之大，恰如人各有其貌与其性格之间的差异。有些人开始行动时全无顾忌，却在应该坚持一下时，轻易地松懈下来，并轻易地气馁放弃。有些人是因为满足于他们已完成了世间荣誉所需求的，有些人是没有客观地掌控住他们在困难面前的怯懦。还有一些人是放任自己败阵于恐慌的心理，另一些人向前冲锋是因为他们不敢再驻留于原地；有的人，在小困难、小挫折前表现出极大的勇气，准备着去面对更大更危险的困境。还有的人，在刀光剑影和枪林弹雨前惊慌失措，有些人在火枪弹药前无所畏惧，却害怕真刀实剑的肉搏战。所有这些不同种类的勇气在某种意义上说是彼此一致的。黑暗通过增加恐惧和遮掩那些好的和坏的行为，给了人们自我宽恕的理由。我们还能观察到世间有一种更常见的情况——我们从未见过真有其人——他总是在确信自己保证不受惩罚的情况下做他最该做的所有的事，因此，对死亡的恐惧略微使他的英勇打了折扣。

216

完全的英勇，拿不出可以向全世界展示的证据。

217

英勇无畏乃是一种源自灵魂深处的非凡力量，它可使人类的灵魂得以超越种种苦恼和混乱，超越那些在重大险境中有可能引发的种种情绪。正是靠这种非凡的力量，英雄们在那些最突如其来和最险象环生的事件中，得以保持镇定的外形，得以保持他们的理性与判断力，得以保持他们的独立自主。

218

伪善是邪恶向德性所表示的敬意。

219

大多数人参与战争是为了以此保全他们的声誉，

但很少人愿意总是这样冒险，因为这种冒险程度，超过了人们为取得成功所预估的必须的危险。

220

虚荣、耻辱，尤其是气质，常常促使男人得以勇敢，女人得以贞洁。

221

我们不愿失去生命，我们梦想获得荣誉，这使得那些勇士们在死亡面前表现出的机智和技巧，胜过贫穷的乞丐在保留他们仅有财物时的灵活和机智。

222

几乎所有人，在迈入成年门槛之后，无一例外地感受到来自肢体和精神机能的不可避免的衰退。

223

感激之心犹如商人的诚信，这种诚信维系着商业贸易，我们诚信行事，并不是因为觉得自己应该偿清债务，而是为了此后能更容易地找到再贷款给我们的人。

224

所有还清了感情债务的人，决不能因此就洋洋自得地以为自己也值得别人感恩。

225

期待他人对我们所给的恩惠表示感激，但错误地估价了这种感激之情的分量，这是因为施予者的骄傲和承受者的自尊在恩惠的价格上意见未能达成一致。

226

偿清某项债务后，那种过分渲染和迫不及待的昭彰之心，正是忘恩负义的一种表现。

227

幸运的人根本不会改正自身错误，当他们的恶行和愚蠢也有好运气相助时，他们会自始至终认为自己是正确无误的。

228

人若骄傲，将不会欠债；人若自爱，当不会还账。

229

过去我们曾受惠于某人，现在，我们原谅了他对我们犯下的罪恶。

230

再没有什么比榜样更富有感染力了，我们所行的一切大善大恶都不过是仿效他人。我们通过效法以模仿好的行为，通过我们本性中的不善而模仿坏的行为，如果没有坏榜样的引导，这种恶意本不会表现出来。

231

永远明智不犯错，这是最大的错误想法。

232

无论我们给悲痛以何种托辞，但引起悲痛的往往不过是利益和虚荣。

233

悲痛中存有各种形态的伪善，其中一种伪善是：借口哀悼与我们很亲近的一个人的死亡，我们所哀伤的对象实际是我们自己，我们哀伤他对我们作出的好评价，哀伤因他的死亡造成的我们的慰藉、快乐和报酬的遗失。同时，死者还因生者的流泪而有了好名声，即使这眼泪并不是为死者而流。我认为，这是一种处于悲痛中的人们的自欺欺人的伪善。还有另一种虚伪，却没有如此的清白无辜了，因为它强行贯穿于整个世界中，它是那些对显赫而不朽的荣耀所表示出的痛苦。时光于流逝中，已湮没了他们曾有过的所有悲痛之情，但他们仍然坚持不懈地继续淌落泪水，悲声呻吟或者悲切哀叹，他们脸上戴着一副伤痛凝重的表情，他们通过自己所有的行为，以使别人信服：他们的撕心裂肺的悲痛将会一直持续到生命终止之时，除此以外决无停止的可能。这种忧伤愁绪和让人厌烦的虚荣心，常常在矫情做作的女人们那里发现，由于她们的女性性别已经关闭了所有能使她们通向荣耀的通途那样，她们就拼命表现出她们处于伤心至死、无法释怀的剧烈悲痛之情中，以此为自己博取另一种名声。然而，还有另外一种形式的眼泪，其来源不够丰盈，它很容易滑落，也很容易枯竭：为了获取仁慈多情的名声而哭泣，为了获得他人怜悯而哭泣，为了变得悲伤哀叹而哭泣，事实上，还有一种哭泣仅仅是为了避免哭不出的羞耻而哭！

234

人们始终在立场观点上冥顽不化彼此对立的原因，更多的因素是出于骄傲而非出于无知，我们发现优先的位置已经被别人先占了，而我们又不愿甘居下风。

235

我们最容易地向朋友们的苦难与不幸表示安慰时，就是当我们付出的安慰可以有效地证明在向他们施与仁慈的时候。

236

看来，当我们倾情为他人工作时，即使是自爱也会受到善良的欺骗，以至看似我们忘掉了自我的存在；然而，这不过是为了顺利达到目的地而精心选取的一条捷径，它在施与的名义下发放高利贷；它用最为狡猾和精巧的方式赢得一切。

237

如果一个人没有足够的行恶的力量，单纯凭他的善良还不足以受到世人景仰，所有其他形式的善良，最经常的不过是因为他们懒惰无为或者因为他们意志力的薄弱无能。

238

对大多数人行善太多会比对他们一味行恶更为危险。

239

再没有比一味盲从大人物更为自负的了，其奉承的程度超过自傲，因为我们把这种盲从视为我们自身价值的成果，而忘记那往往是出于我们的虚荣心，抑或是出于我们无力保持谨言慎行。

240

我们可以说，一个人身上与美貌迥异的那种协调一致的魅力，乃是某种我们尚不知道规则的均衡和对称之美，是一种存在于此人的各种外表特征之间的神秘的和谐之美，这种和谐之美还存在于特征、气色和外部形象之间。

242

调情可勾引起女人的本能，并不是所有人都极力与女人去调情，那些人有的是受到恐惧敬畏的束缚，有的则是受到感官及理性的阻止。

在我们自认为最不可能烦扰他人时，我们经常使他人烦扰。

243

几乎没有什么事情是注定不可能实现的，要使它们向我们臣服更主要的是依赖于我们自身努力，而非借助某些技巧。

244

至高无上的精明，是在于熟知各类事物的价值。

245

最为伟大的能力，在于韬光养晦，在于知道如何将自己的实力深藏不露。

246

看似慷慨的行为，经常只是一种伪装的野心，它蔑视那些蝇头小利，以为随后博取较大的利益。

247

大多数人的忠诚，仅仅是吸引他人信任自己的一种自爱手段，一种使自己高居他人之上的方法，一种成为那些最重要秘密的保管人的方法。

248

崇高以轻视一切，而赢得一切。

249

表现为人的声调、眼睛和气度仪态中的雄辩，并不亚于表现为语言修辞方面的雄辩。

250

真正的雄辩在于说出所有应该说的，而不是说出所有可以说的。

251

有一些人因他们的缺点而自我成就，另一些人却因他们的德行而失宠蒙羞。

252

一个人改变趣味轻而易举，而改变癖好却难之又难。

253

利益在幕后推动着所有种类的德行和恶行。

254

谦卑往往只是一种装模作样的顺从,人们利用它来排挤掉别人。谦虚还是"骄傲"的一种诡计,它以退为进,以贬求扬。骄傲的形式虽然千般面孔,却没有任何一种能比隐藏在谦卑的形象下更具隐蔽性和欺骗性的了。

255

所有情感都有其特定的声调、姿势和面孔,正是情感自身的和谐统一,或好或坏、或愉快或不愉快地,使人们因这情感而倍觉愉悦或者憎恶。

256

在所有职业中,每种职业都或多或少地装扮出某种面孔,人们以自我预期的样子粉墨登场。因此,这个世界不过是由众多的演员组成的大舞台而已。

257

庄重严肃的举止,是人们发明出来的一种身体姿态,这姿势可以恰当地掩饰住人内心的真实世界。

258

良好的品味更多来自判断力而非理性。

259

爱情之乐趣,蕴于爱情本身;人们体验这种感情时的快乐与陶醉,会比激发爱情时所得之快乐还要多。

260

彬彬有礼不过是一种愿望——希望别人也同样礼貌对待自己,希望自己被视为文雅有教养。

261

青年人平常接受的教育,不过是以另一种自爱的方式来激励他们前进。

262

在"爱情"中,没有任何激情能像"自爱"那样富于支配性,"自爱"总是蕴谋损害被爱的人的安宁，蕴谋在那里掀起更大的波澜。

263

被称之为"慷慨"，往往不过是赠予者的虚荣心，人们对这种虚荣心花费的心思，远远超过自己所赠送出去的东西。

264

同情心往往是对表现在别人身上的我们自己罪恶的一种反应。它是对我们今后有可能遭到的不幸的一种缜密的深谋远虑，我们给他人以同情心，其实是为了今后在相似情境下帮助我们自己。恰当地说，我们给予他人的同情心，乃是一种事先为我们自己安排的好处。

265

精神世界的褊狭导致顽冥不化，使得人们难以相信超出他们视线之外的东西。

266

如果相信世间存在一种如野心和爱情那般猛烈的、可以击败其他感情的激情，那不过是我们自欺欺人的想法。就连懒惰也不例外。懒惰闲散是那样的衰弱无力、无所事事，却仍不会在做主宰的地位自甘失败，它挑战并篡夺生活中所有意图和行动的权威，以不为人察觉的方式不容置疑地摧毁和耗尽人们所有的激情和德行。

267

未经充分的考察就迅速地认定罪行存在，这是人们的傲慢和懒惰在作怪，人们希望尽快发现罪证，但又不想因为调查罪行而给自己招来麻烦。

268

我们心怀卑鄙的动机，相信别人对那些微不足道事物的判决，可是，我们又不希望自己的名望和荣誉也有赖于这些人的裁决，这些与我们是完全对立的——要么是因为他们的嫉妒，要么是因为他们的成见，或者因为他们才智匮乏——为了让那些人的判决符合我们的心意，我们不惜浪费大量的安宁和生活去冒险。

269

没有人能有足够的智慧认识到自己做的坏事。

270

赢得了一项荣誉,即可保证获得更多荣誉。

271

青春时代,是持续不断的自我陶醉,是理性的高度亢奋。

272

没有什么可使已赢得他人盛誉的人感觉羞辱,就像他们不必采取细微的手段获取利益。

273

世上有些获得他人褒誉的人,这些人在日常事件中多行卑劣之举,且在这卑劣的背后,并不包含任何德行。

274

新妙新奇之于爱情,就像花儿之于果实;它闪烁着美丽夺目的光彩,但这光彩却稍纵即逝且永不再现。

275

天性纯良,显然被世人过分鼓吹、抬得过高了,它往往因一些蝇头小利的困扰而窒息。

276

消减扑灭最为渺小的激情，增加强化那伟大的激情吧，就像风儿吹熄了蜡烛之微光，却吹旺炉火的熊熊烈焰。

277

当女人们还没有爱的时候，她们总认为自己在爱。一段风流韵事，一份多愁善感引发的情怀，一种天生对被宠爱的偏见，一种拒绝爱情时的艰难，统统说服她们，使她们相信她们拥有真正的爱情——其实那不过是轻薄调情而已。

278

通常使我们常常不满意那些调解人的原因是：他们几乎总是为了调解成功而置朋友利益于不顾，因为他们所渴望的是在自己的职业生涯中获取好名声。

279

当我们把朋友们对我们的柔和温顺过分夸大时，

往往不是出于对朋友们的感激之情，而是为了大肆渲染并表现我们自己拥有的德行。

280

我们不吝赞美那些涉世之初的年轻人，是因为我们看到了他们的嫉妒，对早已在社会上有所成就的人们的嫉妒。

281

骄傲，既激起我们对他人的嫉妒心，也不断地帮我们缓和它。

282

有些谎言伪装得比真理还像真理，以至我们没有受骗可能是因为我们判断有误。

283

许多时候，知晓如何利用他人的好建议所需要的才智，并不比给出好建议所需的才智少。

284

世上有这样一种邪恶之人，当他们完全没有善念时，他们对人的危害性反而会小一些。

285

"宽宏大量"被它的名字定义得清清楚楚，然而仍可以说它是一种骄傲的良好感觉，是一种得到他人颂扬的最高尚的方法。

286

再次去爱那个我们已经不再爱的人，令人难以忍受。

287

在同一个事件上我们可以发现许多解决的办法，这并非精神为我们提供的丰富选择，而是智慧的不足——它使我们在想象力所激发出的情景面前踌躇不前，还阻止我们远离了最早也最正确的判断。

288

有些疾病，在某些特定时候用药物治疗反而会促其恶化，最明智的做法在于搞清楚什么时候用药是危险的。

289

假装单纯乃是一种精巧骗术。

290

脾气和精神相比,有更多的缺陷瑕疵。

291

人的德行就像庄稼一样,有其季节性。

292

可以说,人们的性情就像一些建筑物一样,它有各种不同的外观,有些人看了会喜欢认可,另一些人见了会心生厌恶。

293

节制,既不能向对立面索取,也不能克服其野心:节制与野心,二者不可能并存。节制是灵魂的衰弱无力和懒惰怠慢,野心则是灵魂的兴奋剂和动力源。

294

我们总是喜欢那些崇拜我们的人,而无法总是喜欢那些我们崇拜的人。

295

人们确实未能认清自己所有的希冀。

296

爱那些我们不尊敬的人是困难的，但是，爱那些我们尊敬的人也同样困难，尤其是当我们对他们的尊敬超过我们对自己的尊敬时。

297

身体的气质按通常的路线和规则在潜移默化地推动着我们的意愿，把它们聚集到一起，持续对我们施加一种连续和隐秘的支配，以致在我们浑然不觉时，它已在我们的所有行动中都扮演着重要的角色，起着重要的作用。

298

大多数人的感激之情，仅仅是一种想得到更大恩惠的隐秘欲望。

299

几乎所有人都能欣然偿还那些琐碎的小债务；

许多人对那些小恩小惠表现得感恩戴德，可是，在那些伟大的恩惠面前，几乎没有人不忘恩负义！

300

有些荒唐的傻事，会像传染病一样四处蔓延。

301

许多人蔑视财富，但很少有人知道如何更好地利用它。

302

仅仅是在一些价值不大的事情上，我们才敢作敢为而未被假象迷惑。

303

无论是怎样的优良品德被加诸我们身上，我们自己并没有发现这里面有什么新东西。

304

人们可以宽容那些烦扰到自己的人；却不能宽容那些被自己烦扰的人。

305

利益总因人们的恶行而遭到谴责，其实，它更应该因促成人们的善行而受赞美。

306

当我们能够施与他人恩惠时，我们几乎找不到忘恩负义的人。

307

一个人有时有些傲慢自负是恰当的，在群体中仍这么做则是荒谬可笑的。

308

"节制"是人工发明的德行，它可以限制伟大人物们的野心，也可以抚慰那些运气和能力都很少的平庸人。

309

有些人命中注定是白痴，他们做种种傻事不仅是出于自己的抉择，命运也强迫他们那样做。

310

人们在生活中时常遇到一些意外情况,人们只有糊涂一些才能平安脱身。

311

假如有些人从来没有表现出愚蠢,那是因为从没有近距离地仔细查找他们的毛病。

312

情人们从不彼此厌倦,因为他们的话题永远是他们自己。

313

我们的记忆力是多么好啊,能清楚地记得我们所经历过的最为琐碎之事;我们的记忆力又是多么的不好啊,总记不住我们经常把这些琐事讲给同一个人听!

314

我们谈论自己时的那种过分狂喜,应该提醒我们注意到这样一个事实:那些听众并没有用心倾听,没有与我们共享快乐。

315

能阻止人们向朋友透露自己内心隐私的，通常不是对朋友们的不信任，而是对自己的不信任。

316

意志脆弱的人难以保持真诚。

317

施惠于忘恩负义者只是小小的不幸，被一个无赖小人施与好处，才是真正让人难以承受的大灾祸。

318

我们可以找到医治白痴之傻病的方法，却没有任何良策能矫正灵魂的乖戾。

319

一旦有权利细想朋友们和恩人们的缺点，我们就无法再对他们抱应该抱有的感情。

320

盛赞君主们并不具备的那些德行，实际上是用一种不受处罚的方法责备他们。

321

有的人爱我们，超过了我们的预期；有些人恨我们。二者相较，我们更接近后一种人。

322

只有那些可鄙之人，才会害怕被人鄙视。

323

我们的智慧和我们的财物一样受命运的支配。

324

嫉妒中包括的自爱比爱情中包括得还多。

325

我们常常通过向恶行示弱来自我缓解痛苦，这是因为理性没有足够的力量慰藉我们。

326

嘲笑他人不体面，比自身不体面更甚。

327

我们承认自身有小缺陷,只是为了说服他人相信我们没有大毛病。

328

嫉妒之心比憎恨之心,更富矛盾性。

329

有时候我们自认为厌恶谄媚之举——我们不过是讨厌谄媚的那种方式罢了。

330

我们的宽恕心取决于我们爱的深浅程度。

331

我们在幸福时比受虐时更难对情人保持忠贞。

332

女人没有认识到她们所拥有的调情能力。

333

女人不会十足严厉,除非她们心生憎恨。

334

女人若克服调情，比克服爱情还难。

335

在爱情中，谎言欺骗总是比猜忌怀疑走得更远。

336

有这样一种爱情，爱到极致可阻抑猜忌的产生。

337

某些好的品质就像理性，那些想得到它们的人，既无法感知到它们，也不能理解它们。

338

当我们的憎恨之情过甚时，它会把我们降格到憎恨对象之下。

339

人们根据自爱的程度来赏罚自己的善和恶。

340

大多数女人的智慧，只会让她们更加疯狂愚蠢而非更加理性。

341

青年人虽然热情激昂,但是跟老年人的冷静相比,并非更倾向于冒险。

342

来自祖国的母语口音,不仅居于语言之中,也居于人的心灵和精神之中。

343

要想成为伟大人物,人们应在命运的任何境况下都知道如何为自己谋利。

344

大多数人就像植物一样,有一些隐蔽的特性有待他人偶然发现。

345

机会使我们认识他人,却极少认识自己。

346

如果一个女人的情绪无法控制,也就没有什么能控制她的思想和她的心了。

347

除了那些和我们意见相同的人以外,我们再也找不到有理智的人了。

348

恋爱的时候最容易怀疑自己最信任的人。

349

爱情的最大奇迹在于它杜绝了调情。

350

我们之所以满怀痛苦地憎恨那些欺骗我们的人,是因为他们认为他们比我们聪明。

351

当人们不再相爱而想绝交时,又会有许多困难与痛苦。

352

有些人不许别人厌倦,可和这样的人在一起我们倍觉厌倦。

353

处于爱情中的正派人,可能会像个疯子,但不会像野兽那样。

354

世间有某些缺点,它们被装扮得闪闪发光,比德行更有光彩。

355

由于失去朋友,我们有时会遗憾多于悲伤;而对另一些朋友的失去,我们只有悲伤,不会有遗憾。

356

通常,我们只赞美那些景仰我们的人。

357

卑微的精神总易被小事物击败,伟大的精神目睹一切小事物而未受其侵害。

358

谦卑乃是基督伦理中德行的真正标志，没有谦卑，我们会延续所有的缺点毛病，会让那些缺点被骄傲所遮蔽，别人看不到，我们自己也看不到。

359

不忠会毁掉爱情，并且，当人们有嫉妒的理由时就决不能减少嫉妒。值得被人嫉妒的人无法逃避被嫉妒。

360

我们因别人对我们的小小不忠而倍觉耻辱，这耻辱的程度远远超过我们对别人做重大的不义之事时。

361

嫉妒总是与爱一起产生，但很少与爱同时消失。

362

大多数女人为她们的情人之死而痛哭流涕，不是因为爱他们的缘故，而是为了显示她们值得他们宠爱。

363

我们施于别人的恶行,常常不觉得像施给自己的恶行那么严重。

364

我们都相当清楚,总是谈论我们的妻子可不是什么高雅的品味;但我们不太知道,总是谈论自己,会导致同样的效果。

365

有些与生俱来的优良品性会退化为恶行,另一些后天获得的优良品性又不够完美。例如,由理性来教会我们如何规划我们的财产和自信,同时,由本性赋予我们仁慈和勇敢。

366

无论我们多么不相信那些谈论我们的人所表示出的真诚,我们总是认为他们对我们说的话比对别人说的更真实。

367

很少有正派女子不厌倦自己的正派生活。

368

大多数正派女子就像那些隐藏的财宝,她们得以平安自保是因为没有人搜寻到她们。

369

我们为逃避爱情而强加于自身的虐行,往往比我们的爱人带给我们的痛苦还要残忍。

370

几乎没有多少怯懦之人能完全知晓他所害怕的是什么。

371

那些热恋着的人几乎总要犯这样的过错:他没有注意到对方不知何时已不再爱他。

372

大多数年轻人当自己只剩下粗野和无礼的时候,还自以为这是很自然的。

373

人们的眼泪在欺骗了别人之后,紧接着便欺骗自己。

374

如果认为爱自己的情人是因为她爱我们,这简直是个大骗局。

375

平庸之人常常谴责声讨那些超越他们智力范围的事物。

376

嫉妒被真正的友谊摧毁,调情被真正的爱情消灭。

377

洞察力的最大缺点不是中途遇阻,而是走得太远。

378

我们可以给他人以忠告,却不能激发任何行动。

379

当人们的品格衰退时,趣味也随之下降。

380

命运使我们的德行和罪恶昭然若揭,就如同光线使物体显形那样。

381
为了继续对爱人保持忠诚，我们承受着种种挣扎，这一点儿也不比背信强。

382
我们的行为就像给无韵的素体诗押韵，每个人都能把它们放进他满意的结构模式里。

383
谈论自己和把我们愿给别人看的那些缺点亮出来的欲望，构成了我们的真诚的一大部分。

384
只有一点值得我们惊讶，那就是：我们竟然一直能够感到惊讶。

385
在一个人拥有太多的爱的时候让其感觉知足，或者在他拥有太少的爱的时候让其满足，是同等困难的。

386

没有什么人能比那些不能容忍别人犯错误的人更经常犯错误。

387

愚笨之人缺乏足够的资质以使自己变得优秀。

388

即使虚荣没有完全颠覆各种德行,它至少使它们摇摇欲坠。

389

别人的虚荣心之所以使我们痛苦难耐,是因为它伤害到了我们自己的虚荣心。

390

人们改变兴趣比改变品味要容易得多。

391

命运极度盲目,再没有谁比那些她从没给过好处的人更清楚了。

392

人们应当像对待身体健康那样把握命运：当命运不错时就充分享用；厄运连连时就忍耐，若非陷入绝境，决不要做重大的矫正。

393

笨拙不雅，有时在军营中消失不见，但决不会在宫廷中消失。

394

一个人经常比另一个人机智，但他决不会比所有人都机智。

395

许多时候，被爱人欺骗很痛苦，但从这欺骗中醒悟过来，往往会更痛苦。

396

我们会长久地爱着初恋情人——如果我们还没有找到第二个情人。

397

我们通常没有勇气说自己没有瑕疵、完美无缺，也没有勇气说我们的敌人一无是处；但在事实上，我们所做的和所想的相去甚远。

398

在人们所有的缺点中，最为人们欣然接受的缺点是懒惰：我们相信它会使所有的德行失去效力，相信它完全不会摧毁德行，它顶多只是延缓了其操作实施而已。

399

有一种完全不依赖于命运的高尚：它是一种使我们与众不同的确定的神态举止，它似乎预定将赋予我们伟大事业，这是一种我们不知不觉地自我赋予的价值，正是通过这种优秀品质，我们赢得了别人的尊重，也正是它常常使我们超越了那些出身、等级甚至德行本身。

400

也许存在没有职位的天才，但没有哪个职位能离开各式各样的天才而存在。

401

等级地位之于德行,恰似衣着装扮之于女人。

402

在调情时,爱情的成分最少。

403

命运有时会利用我们的缺陷提升我们;有些叫人厌烦的人,如果我们不想替他们出席的话,他们就不会得到好报。

404

看来,本性是潜藏在我们心灵深处的不为我们所知的各种才智和能力,有能力揭开它面纱的只有激情,并且,许多时候本性会向我们展示出最为真实、精妙的各类见解和图景。

405

我们毫无经验地抵达人生的不同时期,而且,无论我们在哪个年龄段抵达哪个时期,我们总是缺少那一时期的经验。

406

卖弄风情的女人为维护脸面必须做的事是：嫉妒情人们，并掩盖她对其他女人的羡慕。

407

那些身陷我们诡计圈套的人，看起来远非我们所预期的那么愚蠢，一点儿也不像我们中了别人诡计时所表现出的那种愚蠢。

408

上了年纪的、曾经惹人爱的人，最危险的荒唐事莫过于忘记了自己已经不再可爱。

409

我们应该为自己最好的善举时时感到羞耻——如果世人只看动机的话。

410

友谊的最大成绩，不是把我们的缺点暴露给朋友，而是引导他看到自己的缺点。

411

比起我们为数不多的缺点来说,最不可原谅的事是我们掩盖这些缺点的手段。

412

无论人们受到什么样的耻辱,人们几乎总是有能力重塑自己的品性。

413

智力单薄之人难以保持长久的愉悦。

414

傻瓜和疯子,只通过他们自己的才智来观察世界。

415

才智有时候可以帮助我们不受惩罚地做一些粗暴无礼的事。

416

人们年迈苍苍时所增加的活泼性情,总少不了有荒唐与之相伴。

417

情人相爱时，那个爱得最快的人，也总是失恋后痊愈得最好的。

418

不愿表现为风骚放荡的少女，和不想显得荒谬可爱的老人，在谈论爱情之时，绝不应该像谈论一件他们可以谋取利益的事那样。

419

人们能够在一个低于自己能力的职位上大显身手，但在一个高于自己能力的职位上却卑微无为。

420

我们经常认为，当处于一无所有且身份受损的不幸中时，我们有一种不屈不挠的精神；我们经受苦难，并且不会把它视为任人宰割的胆小鬼。

421

思想比智慧在会谈沟通时更有助益。

422

所有的激情都促使我们做各种错事，而爱情自己就能使我们做出荒谬之事。

423

很少有人懂得如何变老。

424

我们经常把自己的缺点看做与他们相反的东西，因此，在我们软弱的时候，便吹嘘说自己是不好惹的。

425

洞察力有一副预言家的神气，它比精神的其他特性都更能满足我们的虚荣心。

426

新颖的魅力和陈旧的习惯，尽管它们彼此对立，却同样地蒙上了我们的双眼，使我们看不到朋友的缺点。

427

大多数朋友使我们对友谊充满厌倦，大多数虔诚者使我们对虔诚倍感厌恶。

428

我们很容易原谅那些没有被我们觉察到有缺点的朋友。

429

处在爱恋中的女人，欣欣然地原谅那些重大的冒失，竟比原谅那些小小的不忠诚还要容易。

430

爱情衰老之时，就像生命衰老时一样，虽然生命已无欢笑可言，我们为了痛苦而继续活下去。

431

没有什么比期望看起来不矫揉造作而更矫揉造作的了。

432

对善行的倾心赞美，就是加入善行行列的一种方式。

433

天生品性崇高之人,最明确的标志是,他们自出生之日起就没有嫉妒心。

434

当朋友欺骗了我们时,我们只需对他们的友谊形式报之以漠然,但我们对他们的不幸却总是相当敏感。

435

命运和性格统治着世界。

436

了解一群人比了解一个人要容易得多。

437

判定一个人的价值,不应该根据他自身固有的品性价值,而应该根据他如何运用自己的这些品性来判定。

438

存在这样一种真实的感激:它不仅使我们从收

受朋友的恩惠中豁免债务，并且把债务转移给我们的朋友，甚至会使我们的朋友倒欠我们。

439
一旦完全知晓我们究竟在渴求什么，那么我们仍存渴求之心的事物就会少而又少了。

440
大多数女人很少为友谊所打动，其原因是：在美妙的爱情之后，任何友谊都平淡无味。

441
常常使我们倍觉幸福的，是未知的事物而非已知的事物，而在恋爱时如此，在交友时也是如此。

442
我们努力把那些坚决不想改正的缺点，变成我们的优点。

443
那些最为猛烈强势的激情，有时会暂时放过我们；但虚荣心却始终与我们纠缠难分。

444

老年人的愚蠢比年轻人的愚蠢更甚。

445

弱点往往比恶行更有害于德行。

446

耻辱心和嫉妒心能极为尖锐地扎痛人们，其原因在于人们的虚荣心无法忍受它们

447

礼节是所有规范中最为微小却最容易让人顺从的规范。

448

理智健全的精神，易于向理智不健全的头脑臣服，而难于引导它变得健全。

449

当命运出人意料地给人们提供一个重要地位后，却没有引导人们继续对它充满期待，也没有给人们

树立起新的希望，人们不可能会长久拥有这个地位，也不可能和这个地位表现得般配得体。

450

我们的骄傲情绪常常因为我们改掉了其他毛病而膨胀。

451

愚蠢之人让人乏味，自认为有智慧的蠢夫更使人厌倦。

452

世界上没有一个人会承认：自己无论何时何处，样样都不如他认为世间最能干的那个人。

453

在重大的事件前，我们不应该枉费心思去创造时机，而应该充分利用现有的条件和机会。

454

在没有被他人指指点点的情况下，我们应该主动放弃某项好处做一件亏本的生意，——这种情境实在罕见。

455

无论这世界如何规划布置，它仍可能是不公正的，它总是宠爱伪善的德行，而非公正地对待真正的德行。

456

我们有时会遇到满腹才智的傻瓜，但从未遇到过富于判断力的傻瓜。

457

向人们展示出我们的真实面孔，会比力图在人前装出某个并不属实的假象，将获益更大。

458

敌人站在他们的立场对我们做出的判断，比我们站在自己立场做出的自我判断，往往更客观准确。

459

确实存在一些能医治爱情的药物，但哪种药也不能保证绝对有效。

460

在知晓了自身所有的激情所导致的一切后果之后，我们才适合有所举措。

461

老年是一个暴君，它禁止了青春时期的所有欢愉乐趣，只因它自己处在一生最痛苦的阶段。

462

骄傲使人们谴责那些自认为已经摆脱了的缺点不足；但同样的骄傲又勾起人们对自己所不具备的优秀品性的蔑视不屑。

463

在我们对敌人的不幸表现出的同情中，骄傲的成分往往比善良的成分更多；它显示出我们对他们是多么的高高在上，我们施舍给他们的是我们的怜悯。

464

世间存在着超出人们理解力的超常之善和超常之恶。

465

如果能像"罪恶"那样善于自我保护,"清白无辜"简直是幸运之极。

466

在所有强烈的感情中,最能使一个女人变好的是爱情。

467

虚荣心比理智更甚,使我们做出更多有违我们品味之事。

468

某些不良的个人品质,却成就了伟大的才智。

469

凡是理性所渴望的,都不是我们真正所渴望的。

470

我们所有的品性都是不确定和不可靠的,无论好品性还是恶品性,它们几乎都是受机遇摆布的傀儡。

471

在最初的激情中,女人所迷恋的是她们的情人;在随后的其他激情中,女人们所爱的乃是爱情本身。

472

像其他的激情那样,骄傲也富于讽刺性。我们因承认自己有嫉妒心而倍觉羞愧,然而我们又因有过这种羞愧和能有这种羞愧而倍觉自豪。

473

真正的爱情何其鲜见,而真正的友谊比真正的爱情更为难求!

474

娇美容颜已去,但魅力犹存,这样的女子实在少之又少。

475

对被同情和被钦佩的渴望,往往是构成我们的信心的最大的部分。

476

我们的嫉妒所持续的时间，总要比我们嫉妒的对象持续好运的时间还要长久。

477

那种可经受过爱情考验的坚强力量，同样也可使经受得起时间和耐力的考验；而那些软弱的人们，往往因激情而兴高采烈，却又几乎从未真正拥有过行动。

478

奇思妙想并不会为我们制造出各种各样的矛盾，因为矛盾天生存在所有人心灵深处。

479

只有那些拥有坚强力量的人，才能拥有真正的温文尔雅。那些仅仅外貌表现为温文尔雅的人，通常不过是软弱脆弱而已，并且这种文雅会很轻易地转变成粗俗不堪。

480

胆怯畏缩是一种缺点，这缺点对我们想纠正的一切事物都有损无益。

481

再没有哪种品性比真正的温厚贤良更鲜见的了，甚至那些相信自己具有这德行之人，通常也不过是出于软弱顺从或者懦弱无力。

482

精神由于闲散懒惰和习性惯性而依附于那些任何能带给它舒适愉快的事物上，这种习性总是为认知能力设置种种界限，没有人愿意付出努力以使自己的精神境界能尽可能地提升和拓展。

483

一般来说，人们的尖酸刻薄主要来自虚荣心而非心怀恶意。

484

当人们的心灵仍因激情倾覆崩坍时的混乱而纷扰时，人们倾向于采纳另一种全新的激情，而不是等待原有激情平复痊愈。

485

那些曾拥有过强烈激情的人们,在激情之伤痊愈后,仍在整整一生中不时感受到激情之痛。

486

心中不存自爱私欲的人,多于心中缺少嫉妒的人。

487

人们有更多的惰性存在于头脑中,而非肢体上。

488

人们情绪的平静安宁或躁动不安,并不是取决于人们在生活中所遇到的那些相当重要的事件的多少,而是取决于人们对日常生活中的琐屑之事的处理是明智正确,还是处理不当。

489

无论是多么邪恶不道德之人,他们仍不敢公然地表现为德行的敌人,当他们想做损害德行之事时,他们要么粉墨登场假装信服德行的不足之处,或者干脆把某种德行归类为罪行。

490

我们经常从爱情走向野心,却极少由野心走回到爱情。

491

贪婪过度几乎意味着一贯的错误,因为它既没有激情以抛开烙在自己身上的标签,也没有能力将那会对未来造成损失的力量制于麾下。

492

贪婪往往产生相互对立的后果:很多人为了某个不确定的遥远的期待,而不惜献出他们拥有的财物;另一些人却为了眼前的蝇头小利而错过将来的大好前程。

493

看起来人们没有觉察到自己的缺点已经足够多,因为人们仍通过某些确定的品性奇特的东西呈现自己,他们满怀强烈的、一丝不苟的精神精心培植这些东西,以致让它们变成本质缺点,变成他们难以纠正的缺点。

494

当别人评述到自己的所作所为时，使我们觉得他们从无过错或瑕疵不足，这一现象使我们领会到：人们往往比我们想象的更清楚自己的缺点；那个使他们短视并失去判断力的"自爱"，也会开启他们的心智，给予他们非常准确的观察力，这种观察力使他们能抑制或者伪装起那些有可能给他们带来他人非议的最不起眼的小毛病。

495

年轻人开始涉世时，应该是腼腆不安的，或者是大胆冒失的；庄重严肃和稳重老成的神态往往会变质为不合时宜的愚蠢失礼。

496

假如争吵的双方只有一方有错，那么争吵很快就会偃旗息鼓。

497

对一个女人而言，如果她拥有青春年少但美貌不足，或者她拥有花容月貌却人老珠黄，都是没有身价的。

498

有些人过于轻佻妄动或者浮躁薄情，以致他们像远离了顽固的缺点过失那样，也远离了坚定的品性德行。

499

如果一个女人不是第二次调情时为人们所知，人们通常不会猜测到她有过第一次调情行为。

500

有些人完全被自我所充盈，甚至在他们恋爱时，也不过是找到了一种让自己的激情而非爱人充盈自身的做法。

501

无论爱情有多么令人愉快惬意，它得以取悦于人的更多原因是其方式技能而非它自身的魅力。

502

那些富于才智性情乖张的人，要比那些虽才智有限但判断力强且直截了当的人，更容易招致他人厌烦。

503

嫉妒在所有过错中位居榜首，它使得人们对嫉妒者本人给予的怜悯也最少。

504

在论及表面德行的虚假性以后，现在该谈谈与蔑视死亡之虚假性有关的道理了，在这里，我的意思是特指异教徒那种对来世不抱希望、不存期待，而一味鼓吹可借自身意志力即可做到的对死亡的蔑视。英勇无畏地与死亡交锋，和高高在上地蔑视死亡，二者存有区别，前者相当常见，而后者我认为是伪装出来的。然而，无以计数的所有相关文字被人们激情写出，用以说服我们相信"死亡不是灾祸"的观点，最意志薄弱之人和最英勇胆大之人平等地站在一起，枚举无数经典事例来强化这种意识，但我仍然怀疑那些判断力极佳的人们会真的信服这种论调。人们承受着种种苦难与磨砺，以求能像说服自己那样说服他人，这苦难与磨砺足以证明那种说服绝非轻而易举之事。人们也许会有种种理由厌倦生命,但绝无任何理由蔑视生命,甚至那些自愿赴死的人也不能把死亡视为轻松之举——如果死亡以一种与他们所选定的方式不同的姿态不期而至时,他们会和世间其他人一样,充满同样的恐惧惊慌,充满同样的震惊骇然。人们注意到的数量繁多的英勇之士们所体现出的勇气时有差异,这是由于死亡之路与他们所想象的有所不同,死亡会在某一个时刻比另一个时刻表现得更为鲜明迫近。因此,在勇士们忽视了死亡之时,他们表现得蔑视死亡;当他们对即将到来的死亡有所知晓时,他们最终害怕死亡。如果人们能够得以避免直面死亡,并避开各种死亡情境,那么也许人们会相信死亡并非最大的灾祸。最贤明理智和最英勇无畏之人,是那些善于使用最恰当的办法避免自己反复思索死亡的人,而所有知晓死亡、看到死亡之影的人们却视死亡为极为可怖之事。死亡的必然性造就了哲学家们的全部坚定性。他们认为,如果不能阻止死亡不断前来的步履,如果不能延长充满不确定性的生命,那么最明智的做法就是以优雅的姿态迎接死亡。纵使身后无物可以延续,却能竖立起道德的丰碑,能在这最具普遍性的灾难中留存一切可存之物。为在死亡面前有能力做出一副从容的表情,不再讨论关乎我们自身的一切，让我们更多地寄希望于人们的天性本能而非那些容易犯错的理性吧，这容易犯错的理性使人们误以为我们能够满不在乎地接近死亡。英勇赴死时的荣光，倍觉懊悔时的期望，留得死后好名声的心愿，从悲惨生活中解脱，不再任由诡谲命运摆布的担保，这一切都是我们面对死亡时，不可忽视的心灵支撑，但我们也不能就此认为这些灵魂支撑是万无一失的。它们为保护我们所起的作用就像一个可为人们遮蔽身体的简单屏障物，这个屏障物在战争的枪林弹雨中可用以冲向堡垒时防身。当我们离堡垒还很远时，人们断定它可能是个很好的掩护；可当人们靠近它时，才发现它不过是自己最为软弱无力的援助物。当距离死亡还有一段距离时，人们认为可以避险，当死亡逼近人们时，那情形和在远处判断已迥然相异；如果人们认为那只是自己脆弱的情感，自然而然地认为拥有在最严峻的考验下也不垮倒的力量，这些都不过是自欺欺人而已。死亡如同自爱，能促使人们把那些必然要摧毁它的东西看得无足轻重，这无疑是对自爱效用的一种错误认识；至于那些我们认为能从中获得力量源泉的理性，它在这场战斗中却懦弱无力，不能按人们的意愿以人们所预期的方式说服人们。由于理性非常频繁地背信弃义，它非但没能激起人们对死亡的蔑视，反而向人们展示出死亡所有的可怕和恐怖。理性为我们所能做到的全部，只不过是劝告我们把视线转移到其他目标上。罗马政治家加图和布鲁图斯选择的是彪炳史册的做法。不久之前，当一个男仆即将被处罚以车轮刑时，他自得地在断头台上跳起舞来。虽然驱动人们的动机各有不同，但最终的结局却是一样。至于其他，尽管在伟大人物和普通大众之间无论存在何种差异，人们已在持续数千载的历史中看到这两种人以同样的镇定自如迎接死亡。然而，那种差异仍然存在：伟大人们所表现出的对死亡的蔑视，只是因为他们对名望之珍爱，这种对名望之爱使他们置生死于度外；而普通人表现出的对死亡的蔑视，是由于他们的头脑肤浅、眼界狭隘，使他们看不见不幸的程度，使他们不能对其他事物进行自由反省。

Maxims

La Rochefoucauld

Introduction

The description of the "ancien regime" in France, "a despotism tempered by epigrams", like most epigrammatic sentences, contains some truth, with much fiction. The society of the last half of the seventeenth, and the whole of the eighteenth centuries, was doubtless greatly influenced by the precise and terse mode in which the popular writers of that date expressed their thoughts. To a people naturally inclined to think that every possible view, every conceivable argument, upon a question is included in a short aphorism, a shrug, and the word "voilà", truths expressed in condensed sentences must always have a peculiar charm. It is, perhaps, from this love of epigram, that we find so many eminent French writers of maxims. Pascal, De Retz, La Rochefoucauld, La Bruyère, Montesquieu, and Vauvenargues, each contributed to the rich stock of French epigrams. No other country can show such a list of brilliant writers—in England certainly we cannot. Our most celebrated, Lord Bacon, has, by his other works, so surpassed his maxims, that their fame is, to a great measure, obscured. The only Englishman who could have rivalled La Rochefoucauld or La Bruyère was the Earl of Chesterfield, and he only could have done so from his very intimate connexion with France; but unfortunately his brilliant genius was spent in the impossible task of trying to refine a boorish young Briton, in "cutting blocks with a razor".

Of all the French epigrammatic writers La Rochefoucauld is at once the most widely known, and the most distinguished. Voltaire, whose opinion on the century of Louis XIV. is entitled to the greatest weight, says, "One of the works that most largely contributed to form the taste of the nation, and to diffuse a spirit of justice and precision, is the collection of maxims, by Francois Duc de la Rochefoucauld."

This Francois, the second Duc de la Rochefoucauld, Prince de Marsillac, the author of the maxims, was one of the most illustrious members of the most illustrious families among the French noblesse. Descended from the ancient Dukes of Guienne, the founder of the Family Fulk or Foucauld, a younger branch of the House of Lusignan, was at the commencement of the eleventh century the Seigneur of a small town, La Roche, in the Angounois. Our chief knowledge of this feudal lord is drawn from the monkish chronicles. As the benefactor of the various abbeys and monasteries in his province, he is naturally spoken of by them in terms of eulogy, and in the charter of one of the abbeys of Angouleme he is called, "vir nobilissimus Fulcaldus". His territorial power enabled him to adopt what was then, as is still in Scotland, a common custom, to prefix the name of his estate to his surname, and thus to create and transmit to his descendants the illustrious surname of La Rochefoucauld.

From that time until that great crisis in the history of the French aristocracy, the Revolution of 1789, the family of La Rochefoucauld have been, "if not first, in the very first line" of that most illustrious body. One Seigneur served under Philip Augustus against Richard

Coeur de Lion, and was made prisoner at the battle of Gisors. The eighth Seigneur Guy performed a great tilt at Bordeaux, attended (according to Froissart) to the Lists by some two hundred of his kindred and relations. The sixteenth Seigneur Francais was chamberlain to Charles VIII. and Louis XII., and stood at the font as sponsor, giving his name to that last light of French chivalry, Francis I.. In 1515 he was created a baron, and was afterwards advanced to a count, on account of his great service to Francis and his predecessors.

The second count pushed the family fortune still further by obtaining a patent as the Prince de Marsillac. His widow, Anne de Polignac, entertained Charles V. at the family chateau at Verteuil, in so princely a manner that on leaving Charles observed, "He had never entered a house so redolent of high virtue, uprightness, and lordliness as that mansion."

The third count, after serving with distinction under the Duke of Guise against the Spaniards, was made prisoner at St. Quintin, and only regained his liberty to fall a victim to the "bloody infamy" of St. Bartholomew. His son, the fourth count, saved with difficulty from that massacre, after serving with distinction in the religious wars, was taken prisoner in a skirmish at St. Yriex la Perche, and murdered by the Leaguers in cold blood.

The fifth count, one of the ministers of Louis XIII., after fighting against the English and Buckingham at the Ile de Ré, was created a duke. His son Francis, the second duke, by his writings has made the family name a household word.

The third duke fought in many of the earlier campaigns of Louis XIV. at Torcy, Lille, Cambray, and was dangerously wounded at the passage of the Rhine. From his bravery he rose to high favour at Court, and was appointed Master of the Horse (Grand Veneur) and Lord Chamberlain. His son, the fourth duke, commanded the regiment of Navarre, and took part in storming the village of Neerwinden on the day when William III. was defeated at Landen. He was afterwards created Duc de la Rochequyon and Marquis de Liancourt.

The fifth duke, banished from Court by Louis XV., became the friend of the philosopher Voltaire.

The sixth duke, the friend of Condorcet, was the last of the long line of noble lords who bore that distinguished name. In those terrible days of September, 1792, when the French people were proclaiming universal humanity, the duke was seized as an aristocrat by the mob at Gisors and put to death behind his own carriage, in which sat his mother and his wife, at the very place where, some six centuries previously, his ancestor had been taken prisoner in a fair fight. A modern writer has spoken of this murder "as an admirable reprisal upon the grandson for the writings and conduct of the grandfather". But M. Sainte Beuve observes as to this, he can see nothing admirable in the death of the duke, and if it proves anything, it is only that the grandfather was not so wrong in his judgment of men as is usually supposed.

Francis, the author, was born on the 15th December 1615. M. Sainte Beuve divides his life into four periods, first, from his birth till he was thirty-five, when he became mixed up in the war of the Fronde; the second period, during the progress of that war; the third, the twelve years that followed, while he recovered from his wounds, and wrote his maxims during his retirement from society; and the last from that time till his death.

In the same way that Herodotus calls each book of his history by the name of one of the muses, so each of these four periods of La Rochefoucauld's life may be associated with the name of a woman who was for the time his ruling passion. These four ladies are the Duchesse de Chevreuse, the Duchesse de Longueville, Madame de Sablé, and Madame de La Fayette.

La Rochefoucauld's early education was neglected; his father, occupied in the affairs of state, either had not, or did not devote any time to his education. His natural talents and his habits of observation soon, however, supplied all deficiencies. By birth and station placed in the best society of the French Court, he soon became a most finished courtier. Knowing how precarious Court favour then was, his father, when young Rochefoucauld was only nine years old, sent him into the army. He was subsequently attached to the regiment of Auvergne. Though but sixteen he was present, and took part in the military operations at the siege of Cassel. The Court of Louis XIII. was then ruled imperiously by Richelieu. The Duke de la Rochefoucauld was strongly opposed to the Cardinal's party. By joining in the plots of Gaston of Orleans, he gave Richelieu an opportunity of ridding Paris of his opposition. When those plots were discovered, the Duke was sent into a sort of banishment to Blois.

His son, who was then at Court with him, was, upon the pretext of a liaison with Mdlle. d'Hautefort, one of the ladies in waiting on the Queen (Anne of Austria), but in reality to prevent the Duke learning what was passing at Paris, sent with his father. The result of the exile was Rochefoucauld's marriage. With the exception that his wife's name was Mdlle. Vivonne, and that she was the mother of five sons and three daughters, nothing is known of her. While Rochefoucauld and his father were at Blois, the Duchesse de Chevreuse, one of the beauties of the Court, and the mistress of Louis, was banished to Tours. She and Rochefoucauld met, and soon became intimate, and for a time she was destined to be the one motive of his actions. The Duchesse was engaged in a correspondence with the Court of Spain and the Queen. Into this plot Rochefoucauld threw himself with all his energy; his connexion with the Queen brought him back to his old love Mdlle. d'Hautefort, and led him to her party, which he afterwards followed. The course he took shut him off from all chance of Court favour. The King regarded him with coldness, the Cardinal with irritation. Although the Bastile and the scaffold, the fate of Chalais and Montmorency, were before his eyes, they failed to deter him from plotting. He was about twenty-three; returning to Paris, he warmly sided with the Queen. He says in his Memoirs that the only persons she could then trust were himself and Mdlle. d'Hautefort, and it was proposed he should take both of them from Paris to Brussels. Into this plan he entered with all his youthful indiscretion, it being for several reasons the very one he would wish to adopt, as it would strengthen his influence with Anne of Austria, place Richelieu and his master in an uncomfortable position, and save Mdlle. d'Hautefort from the attentions the King was showing her.

But Richelieu of course discovered this plot, and Rochefoucauld was, of course, sent to the Bastile. He was liberated after a week's imprisonment, but banished to his chateau at Verteuil.

The reason for this clemency was that the Cardinal desired to win Rochefoucauld from the Queen's party. A command in the army was offered to him, but by the Queen's orders refused.

For some three years Rochefoucauld remained at Verteuil, waiting the time for his reckoning with Richelieu; speculating on the King's death, and the favours he would then receive from the Queen. During this period he was more or less engaged in plotting against his enemy the Cardinal, and hatching treason with Cinq Mars and De Thou.

M. Sainte Beuve says, that unless we study this first part of Rochefoucauld's life, we shall never understand his maxims. The bitter disappointment of the passionate love, the high hopes then formed, the deceit and treachery then witnessed, furnished the real key to their meaning. The cutting cynicism of the morality was built on the ruins of that chivalrous ambition and romantic affection. He saw his friend Cinq Mars sent to the scaffold, himself betrayed by men whom he had trusted, and the only reason he could assign for these actions was intense selfishness.

Meanwhile, Richelieu died. Rochefoucauld returned to Court, and found Anne of Austria regent, and Mazarin minister. The

Queen's former friends flocked there in numbers, expecting that now their time of prosperity had come. They were bitterly disappointed. Mazarin relied on hope instead of gratitude, to keep the Queen's adherents on his side. The most that any received were promises that were never performed. In after years, doubtless, Rochefoucauld's recollection of his disappointment led him to write the maxim: "We promise according to our hopes, we perform according to our fears." But he was not even to receive promises; he asked for the Governorship of Havre, which was then vacant. He was flatly refused. Disappointment gave rise to anger, and uniting with his old flame, the Duchesse de Chevreuse, who had received the same treatment, and with the Duke of Beaufort, they formed a conspiracy against the government. The plot was, of course, discovered and crushed. Beaufort was arrested, the Duchesse banished. Irritated and disgusted, Rochefoucauld went with the Duc d'Enghein, who was then joining the army, on a campaign, and here he found the one love of his life, the Duke's sister, Mdme. de Longueville. This lady, young, beautiful, and accomplished, obtained a great ascendancy over Rochefoucauld, and was the cause of his taking the side of Condé in the subsequent civil war. Rochefoucauld did not stay long with the army. He was badly wounded at the siege of Mardik, and returned from thence to Paris. On recovering from his wounds, the war of the Fronde broke out. This war is said to have been most ridiculous, as being carried on without a definite object, a plan, or a leader. But this description is hardly correct; it was the struggle of the French nobility against the rule of the Court; an attempt, the final attempt, to recover their lost influence over the state, and to save themselves from sinking under the rule of cardinals and priests.

With the general history of that war we have nothing to do; it is far too complicated and too confused to be stated here. The memoirs of Rochefoucauld and De Retz will give the details to those who desire to trace the contests of the factions—the course of the intrigues. We may confine ourselves to its progress so far as it relates to the Duc de la Rochefoucauld.

On the Cardinal causing the Princes de Condé and Conti, and the Duc de Longueville, to be arrested, Rochefoucauld and the Duchess fled into Normandy. Leaving her at Dieppe, he went into Poitou, of which province he had some years previously bought the post of governor. He was there joined by the Duc de Bouillon, and he and the Duke marched to, and occupied Bordeaux. Cardinal Mazarin and Marechal de la Meilleraie advanced in force on Bordeaux, and attacked the town. A bloody battle followed. Rochefoucauld defended the town with the greatest bravery, and repulsed the Cardinal. Notwithstanding the repulse, the burghers of Bordeaux were anxious to make peace, and save the city from destruction. The Parliament of Bordeaux compelled Rochefoucauld to surrender. He did so, and returned nominally to Poitou, but in reality in secret to Paris.

There he found the Queen engaged in trying to maintain her position by playing off the rival parties of the Prince Condé and the Cardinal De Retz against each other. Rochefoucauld eagerly espoused his old party—that of Condé. In August, 1651, the contending parties met in the Hall of the Parliament of Paris, and it was with great difficulty they were prevented from coming to blows even there. It is even said that Rochefoucauld had ordered his followers to murder De Retz.

Rochefoucauld was soon to undergo a bitter disappointment. While occupied with party strife and faction in Paris, Madame de Chevreuse left him, and formed an alliance with the Duc de Nemours. Rochefoucauld still loved her. It was, probably, thinking of this that he afterwards wrote, "Jealousy is born with love, but does not die with it." He endeavoured to get Madame de Chatillon, the old mistress of the Duc de Nemours, reinstated in favour, but in this he did not succeed. The Duc de Nemours was soon after killed in a duel. The war went on, and after several indecisive skirmishes, the decisive battle was fought at Paris, in the Faubourg St. Antoine, where the Parisians first learnt the use or the abuse of their favourite defence, the barricade. In this battle, Rochefoucauld behaved with great bravery. He was wounded in the head, a wound which for a time deprived him of his sight. Before he recovered, the war was over, Louis XIV. had attained his majority, the gold of Mazarin, the arms of Turenne, had been successful, the French nobility were vanquished, the court supremacy established.

This completed Rochefoucauld's active life.

When he recovered his health, he devoted himself to society. Madame de Sablé assumed a hold over him. He lived a quiet life, and occupied himself in composing an account of his early life, called his "Memoirs", and his immortal "Maxims".

From the time he ceased to take part in public life, Rochefoucauld's real glory began. Having acted the various parts of soldier, politician, and lover with but small success, he now commenced the part of moralist, by which he is known to the world.

Living in the most brilliant society that France possessed, famous from his writings, distinguished from the part he had taken in public affairs, he formed the centre of one of those remarkable French literary societies, a society which numbered among its members La Fontaine, Racine, Boileau. Among his most attached friends was Madame de La Fayette (the authoress of the "Princess of Cleeves"), and this friendship continued until his death. He was not, however, destined to pass away in that gay society without some troubles. At the passage of the Rhine in 1672 two of his sons were engaged; the one was killed, the other severely wounded. Rochefoucauld was much affected by this, but perhaps still more by the death of the young Duc de Longueville, who perished on the same occasion.

Sainte Beuve says that the cynical book and that young life were the only fruits of the war of the Fronde. Madame de Sévigné, who was with him when he heard the news of the death of so much that was dear to him, says, "I saw his heart laid bare on that cruel occasion, and his courage, his merit, his tenderness, and good sense surpassed all I ever met with. I hold his wit and accomplishments as nothing in comparison." The combined effect of his wounds and the gout caused the last years of Rochefoucauld's life to be spent in great pain. Madame de Sévigné, who was with him continually during his last illness, speaks of the fortitude with which he bore his sufferings as something to be admired. Writing to her daughter, she says, "Believe me, it is not for nothing he has moralised all his life; he has thought so often on his last moments that they are nothing new or unfamiliar to him."

In his last illness, the great moralist was attended by the great divine, Bossuet. Whether that matchless eloquence or his own philosophic calm had, in spite of his writings, brought him into the state Madame de Sévigné describes, we know not; but one, or both, contributed to his passing away in a manner that did not disgrace a French noble or a French philosopher. On the 11th March, 1680, he ended his stormy life in peace after so much strife, a loyal subject after so much treason.

One of his friends, Madame Deshoulières, shortly before he died sent him an ode on death, which aptly describes his state— "Oui, soyez alors plus ferme, Que ces vulgaires humains Qui, près de leur dernier terme, De vaines terreurs sont pleins. En sage que rien n'offense, Livrez-vous sans resistance A d'inévitables traits; Et, d'une demarche égale, Passez cette onde fatal Qu'on ne repasse jamais."

Rochefoucauld left behind him only two works, the one, Memoirs of his own time, the other the Maxims. The first described the scenes in which his youth had been spent, and though written in a lively style, and giving faithful pictures of the intrigues and the scandals of the court during Louis XIV.'s minority, yet, except to the historian, has ceased at the present day to be of much interest. It forms, perhaps, the true key to understand the special as opposed to general application of the maxims.

Notwithstanding the assertion of Bayle, that "there are few people so bigoted to antiquity as not to prefer the Memoirs of La Rochefoucauld to the Commentaries of Caesar," or the statement of Voltaire, "that the Memoirs are universally read and the Maxims are learnt by heart," few persons at the present day ever heard of the Memoirs, and the knowledge of most as to the Maxims is confined to that most celebrated of all, though omitted from his last edition, "There is something in the misfortunes of our best friends which does not wholly displease us." Yet it is difficult to assign a cause for this; no book is perhaps oftener unwittingly quoted, none certainly oftener unblushingly pillaged; upon none have so many contradictory opinions been given.

"Few books," says Mr. Hallam, "have been more highly extolled, or more severely blamed, than the maxims of the Duke of Rochefoucauld, and that not only here, but also in France." Rousseau speaks of it as "a sad and melancholy book", though he goes on to say "it is usually so in youth when we do not like seeing man as he is". Voltaire says of it, in the words above quoted, "One of the works which most contributed to form the taste of the (French) nation, and to give it a spirit of justness and precision, was the collection of the maxims of Francois Duc de la Rochefoucauld, though there is scarcely more than one truth running through the book—that 'self-love is the motive of everything'—yet this thought is presented under so many varied aspects that it is nearly always striking. It is not so much a book as it is materials for ornamenting a book. This little collection was read with avidity, it taught people to think, and to comprise their thoughts in a lively, precise, and delicate turn of expression. This was a merit which, before him, no one in Europe had attained since the revival of letters."

Dr. Johnson speaks of it as "the only book written by a man of fashion, of which professed authors need be jealous".

Lord Chesterfield, in his letters to his son, says, "Till you come to know mankind by your experience, I know no thing nor no man that can in the meantime bring you so well acquainted with them as Le Duc de la Rochefoucauld. His little book of maxims, which I would advise you to look into for some moments at least every day of your life, is, I fear, too like and too exact a picture of human nature. I own it seems to degrade it, but yet my experience does not convince me that it degrades it unjustly."

Bishop Butler, on the other hand, blames the book in no measured terms. "There is a strange affectation," says the bishop, "in some people of explaining away all particular affection, and representing the whole life as nothing but one continued exercise of self-love. Hence arise that surprising confusion and perplexity in the Epicureans of old, Hobbes, the author of 'Reflexions Morales', and the whole set of writers, of calling actions interested which are done of the most manifest known interest, merely for the gratification of a present passion."

The judgment the reader will be most inclined to adopt will perhaps be either that of Mr. Hallam, "Concise and energetic in expression, reduced to those short aphorisms which leave much to the reader's acuteness and yet save his labour, not often obscure, and never wearisome, an evident generalisation of long experience, without pedantry, without method, without deductive reasonings, yet wearing an appearance at least of profundity; they delight the intelligent though indolent man of the world, and must be read with some admiration by the philosopher . . . yet they bear witness to the contracted observation and the precipitate inferences which an intercourse with a single class of society scarcely fails to generate." Or that of Addison, who speaks of Rochefoucauld "as the great philosopher for administering consolation to the idle, the curious, and the worthless part of mankind."

We are fortunately in possession of materials such as rarely exist to enable us to form a judgment of Rochefoucauld's character. We have, with a vanity that could only exist in a Frenchman, a description or portrait of himself, of his own painting, and one of those inimitable living sketches in which his great enemy, Cardinal De Retz, makes all the chief actors in the court of the regency of Anne of Austria pass across the stage before us.

We will first look on the portrait Rochefoucauld has left us of himself: "I am," says he, "of a medium height, active, and well-proportioned. My complexion dark, but uniform, a high forehead; and of moderate height, black eyes, small, deep set, eyebrows black and thick but well placed. I am rather embarrassed in talking of my nose, for it is neither flat nor aquiline, nor large; nor pointed: but I believe, as far as I can say, it is too large than too small, and comes down just a trifle too low. I have a large mouth, lips generally red enough, neither shaped well nor badly. I have white teeth, and fairly even. I have been told I have a little too much chin. I have just looked at myself in the glass to ascertain the fact, and I do not know how to decide. As to the shape of my face, it is either square or oval, but which I should find it very difficult to say. I have black hair, which curls by nature, and thick and long enough to entitle me to lay claim to a fine head. I have in my countenance somewhat of grief and pride, which gives many people an idea I despise them, although I am not at all given to do so. My gestures are very free, rather inclined to be too much so, for in speaking they make me use too much action. Such, candidly, I believe I am in outward appearance, and I believe it will be found that what I have said above of myself is not far from the real case. I shall use the same truthfulness in the remainder of my picture, for I have studied myself sufficiently to know myself well; and I will lack neither boldness to speak as freely as I can of my good qualities, nor sincerity to freely avow that I have faults.

"In the first place, to speak of my temper. I am melancholy, and I have hardly been seen for the last three or four years to laugh above three or four times. It seems to me that my melancholy would be even endurable and pleasant if I had none but what belonged to me constitutionally; but it arises from so many other causes, fills my imagination in such a way, and possesses my mind so strongly that for the greater part of my time I remain without speaking a word, or give no meaning to what I say. I am extremely reserved to those I do not know, and I am not very open with the greater part of those I do. It is a fault I know well, and I should neglect no means to correct myself of it; but as a certain gloomy air I have tends to make me seem more reserved than I am in fact, and as it is not in our power to rid ourselves of a bad expression that arises from a natural conformation of features, I think that even when I have cured myself internally, externally some bad expression will always remain.

"I have ability. I have no hesitation in saying it, as for what purpose should I pretend otherwise. So great circumvention, and so great depreciation, in speaking of the gifts one has, seems to me to hide a little vanity under an apparent modesty, and craftily to try to make others believe in greater virtues than are imputed to us. On my part I am content not to be considered better-looking than I am, nor of a better temper than I describe, nor more witty and clever than I am. Once more, I have ability, but a mind spoilt by melancholy, for though I know my own language tolerably well, and have a good memory, a mode of thought not particularly confused, I yet have so great a mixture of discontent that I often say what I have to say very badly.

"The conversation of gentlemen is one of the pleasures that most amuses me. I like it to be serious and morality to form the substance of it. Yet I also know how to enjoy it when trifling; and if I do not make many witty speeches, it is not because I do not appreciate the value of trifles well said, and that I do not find great amusement in that manner of raillery in which certain prompt and ready-witted persons excel so well. I write well in prose; I do well in verse; and if I was envious of the glory that springs from that quarter,

I think with a little labour I could acquire some reputation. I like reading, in general; but that in which one finds something to polish the wit and strengthen the soul is what I like best. But, above all, I have the greatest pleasure in reading with an intelligent person, for then we reflect constantly upon what we read, and the observations we make form the most pleasant and useful form of conversation there is.

"I am a fair critic of the works in verse and prose that are shown me; but perhaps I speak my opinion with almost too great freedom. Another fault in me is that I have sometimes a spirit of delicacy far too scrupulous, and a spirit of criticism far too severe. I do not dislike an argument, and I often of my own free will engage in one; but I generally back my opinion with too much warmth, and sometimes, when the wrong side is advocated against me, from the strength of my zeal for reason, I become a little unreasonable myself.

"I have virtuous sentiments, good inclinations, and so strong a desire to be a wholly good man that my friend cannot afford me a greater pleasure than candidly to show me my faults. Those who know me most intimately, and those who have the goodness sometimes to give me the above advice, know that I always receive it with all the joy that could be expected, and with all reverence of mind that could be desired.

"I have all the passions pretty mildly, and pretty well under control. I am hardly ever seen in a rage, and I never hated any one. I am not, however, incapable of avenging myself if I have been offended, or if my honour demanded I should resent an insult put upon me; on the contrary, I feel clear that duty would so well discharge the office of hatred in me that I should follow my revenge with even greater keenness than other people.

"Ambition does not weary me. I fear but few things, and I do not fear death in the least. I am but little given to pity, and I could wish I was not so at all. Though there is nothing I would not do to comfort an afflicted person, and I really believe that one should do all one can to show great sympathy to him for his misfortune, for miserable people are so foolish that this does them the greatest good in the world; yet I also hold that we should be content with expressing sympathy, and carefully avoid having any. It is a passion that is wholly worthless in a well-regulated mind, which only serves to weaken the heart, and which should be left to ordinary persons, who, as they never do anything from reason, have need of passions to stimulate their actions.

"I love my friends; and I love them to such an extent that I would not for a moment weigh my interest against theirs. I condescend to them, I patiently endure their bad temper. But, also, I do not make much of their caresses, and I do not feel great uneasiness in their absence.

"Naturally, I have but little curiosity about the majority of things that stir up curiosity in other men. I am very secret, and I have less difficulty than most men in holding my tongue as to what is told me in confidence. I am most particular as to my word, and I would never fail, whatever might be the consequence, to do what I had promised; and I have made this an inflexible law during the whole of my life.

"I keep the most punctilious civility to women. I do not believe I have ever said anything before them which could cause them annoyance. When their intellect is cultivated, I prefer their society to that of men: one there finds a mildness one does not meet with among ourselves, and it seems to me beyond this that they express themselves with more neatness, and give a more agreeable turn to the things they talk about. As for flirtation, I formerly indulged in a little, now I shall do so no more, though I am still young. I have renounced all flirtation, and I am simply astonished that there are still so many sensible people who can occupy their time with it.

"I wholly approve of real loves; they indicate greatness of soul, and although, in the uneasiness they give rise to, there is a something contrary to strict wisdom, they fit in so well with the most severe virtue, that I believe they cannot be censured with justice. To me who have known all that is fine and grand in the lofty aspirations of love, if I ever fall in love, it will assuredly be in love of that nature. But in accordance with the present turn of my mind, I do not believe that the knowledge I have of it will ever change from my mind to my heart."

Such is his own description of himself. Let us now turn to the other picture, delineated by the man who was his bitterest enemy, and whom (we say it with regret) Rochefoucauld tried to murder.

Cardinal De Retz thus paints him:— "In M. de la Rochefoucauld there was ever an indescribable something. From his infancy he always wanted to be mixed up with plots, at a time when he could not understand even the smallest interests (which has indeed never been his weak point) or comprehend greater ones, which in another sense has never been his strong point. He was never fitted for any matter, and I really cannot tell the reason. His glance was not sufficiently wide, and he could not take in at once all that lay in his sight, but his good sense, perfect in theories, combined with his gentleness, his winning ways, his pleasing manners, which are perfect, should more than compensate for his lack of penetration. He always had a natural irresoluteness, but I cannot say to what this irresolution is to be attributed. It could not arise in him from the wealth of his imagination, for that was anything but lively. I cannot put it down to the barrenness of his judgment, for, although he was not prompt in action, he had a good store of reason. We see the effects of this irresolution, although we cannot assign a cause for it. He was never a general, though a great soldier; never, naturally, a good courtier, although he had always a good idea of being so. He was never a good partizan, although all his life engaged in intrigues. That air of pride and timidity which your see in his private life, is turned in business into an apologetic manner. He always believed he had need of it; and this, combined with his 'Maxims', which show little faith in virtue, and his habitual custom, to give up matters with the same haste he undertook them, leads me to the conclusion that he would have done far better to have known his own mind, and have passed himself off, as he could have done, for the most polished courtier, the most agreeable man in private life that had appeared in his century."

It is but justice to the Cardinal to say, that the Duc is not painted in such dark colours as we should have expected, judging from what we know of the character of De Retz. With his marvellous power of depicting character, a power unrivalled, except by St. Simon and perhaps by Lord Clarendon, we should have expected the malignity of the priest would have stamped the features of his great enemy with the impress of infamy, and not have simply made him appear a courtier, weak, insincere, and nothing more. Though rather beyond our subject, the character of Cardinal de Retz, as delineated by Mdme. Sévigné, in one of her letters, will help us to form a true conclusion on the different characters of the Duc and the Cardinal. She says:— "Paul de Gondi Cardinal de Retz possesses great elevation of character, a certain extent of intellect, and more of the ostentation than of the true greatness of courage. He has an extraordinary memory, more energy than polish in his words, an easy humour, docility of character, and weakness in submitting to the complaints and reproaches of his friends, a little piety, some appearances of religion. He appears ambitious without being really so. Vanity and those who have guided him, have made him undertake great things, almost all opposed to his profession. He excited the greatest troubles in the State without any design of turning them to account, and far from declaring himself the enemy of Cardinal Mazarin with any view of occupying his place, he thought of nothing but making himself an object of dread to him, and flattering himself with the false vanity of being his rival. He was clever enough, however, to take advantage of the public calamities to get himself made Cardinal. He endured his imprisonment with firmness, and owed his liberty solely to his own daring. In the obscurity of a life of wandering and concealment, his indolence for many years supported him with reputation. He preserved the Archbishopric of Paris against the power of Cardinal Mazarin, but after the death of that minister, he resigned it without knowing what he was doing, and without making use of the opportunity to promote the interests of himself and his friends. He has taken part in several conclaves, and his conduct has always increased his reputation.

"His natural bent is to indolence, nevertheless he labours with activity in pressing business, and reposes with indifference when it is concluded. He has great presence of mind, and knows so well how to turn it to his own advantage on all occasions presented him by fortune, that it would seem as if he had foreseen and desired them. He loves to narrate, and seeks to dazzle all his listeners indifferently by his extraordinary adventures, and his imagination often supplies him with more than his memory. The generality of his qualities are false, and what has most contributed to his reputation is his power of throwing a good light on his faults. He is insensible alike to hatred and to friendship, whatever pains he may be at to appear taken up with the one or the other. He is incapable of envy or avarice, whether from virtue or from carelessness. He has borrowed more from his friends than a private person could ever hope to be able to repay; he has felt the vanity of acquiring so much on credit, and of undertaking to discharge it. He has neither taste nor refinement; he is amused by everything and pleased by nothing. He avoids difficult matters with considerable address, not allowing people to penetrate the slight acquaintance he has with everything. The retreat he has just made from the world is the most brilliant and the most unreal action of his life; it is a sacrifice he has made to his pride under the pretence of devotion; he quits the court to which he cannot attach himself, and retires from a world which is retiring from him."

The Maxims were first published in 1665, with a preface by Segrais. This preface was omitted in the subsequent editions. The first edition contained 316 maxims, counting the last upon death, which was not numbered. The second in 1666 contained only 102; the third in 1671, and the fourth in 1675, 413. In this last edition we first meet with the introductory maxim, "Our virtues are generally but disguised vices." The edition of 1678, the fifth, increased the number to 504. This was the last edition revised by the author, and published in his lifetime. The text of that edition has been used for the present translation. The next edition, the sixth, was published in 1693, about thirteen years after the author's death. This edition included fifty new maxims, attributed by the editor to Rochefoucauld. Most likely they were his writing, as the fact was never denied by his family, through whose permission they were published. They form the third supplement to the translation. This sixth edition was published by Claude Barbin, and the French editions since that time have been too numerous to be enumerated. The great popularity of the Maxims is perhaps best shown from the numerous translations that have been made of them. No less than eight English translations, or so-called translations, have appeared; one American, a Swedish, and a Spanish translation, an Italian imitation, with parallel passages, and an English imitation by Hazlitt. The titles of the English editions are as follows:— i. Seneca Unmasked. By Mrs. Aphara Behn. London, 1689. She calls the author the Duke of Rushfucave. ii. Moral Maxims and Reflections, in four parts. By the Duke de la Rochefoucauld. Now made English. London, 1694. 12 mo. iii. Moral Maxims and Reflections of the Duke de la Rochefoucauld. Newly made English. London, 1706. 12 mo. iv. Moral Maxims of the Duke de la Rochefoucauld. Translated from the French. With notes. London, 1749. 12 mo. v. Maxims and Moral Reflections of the Duke de la Rochefoucauld. Revised and improved. London, 1775. 8 vo. vi. Maxims and Moral Reflections of the Duke de la Rochefoucauld. A new edition, revised and improved, by L. D. London, 1781. 8 vo. vii. The Gentleman's Library. La Rochefoucauld's Maxims and Moral Reflections. London, 1813. 12 mo. viii. Moral Reflections, Sentences, and Maxims of the Duke de la Rochefoucauld, newly translated from the French; with an introduction and notes. London, 1850. 16 mo. ix. Maxims and Moral Reflections of the Duke de la Rochefoucauld: with a Memoir by the Chevalier de Chatelain. London, 1868. 12 mo.

The perusal of the Maxims will suggest to every reader to a greater or less degree, in accordance with the extent of his reading, parallel passages, and similar ideas. Of ancient writers Rochefoucauld most strongly reminds us of Tacitus; of modern writers, Junius most strongly reminds us of Rochefoucauld. Some examples from both are given in the notes to this translation. It is curious to see how the expressions of the bitterest writer of English political satire to a great extent express the same ideas as the great French satirist of private life. Had space permitted the parallel could have been drawn very closely, and much of the invective of Junius traced to its source in Rochefoucauld.

One of the persons whom Rochefoucauld patronised and protected, was the great French fabulist, La Fontaine. This patronage was repaid by La Fontaine giving, in one of his fables, "L'Homme et son Image", an elaborate defence of his patron. After there depicting a man who fancied himself one of the most lovely in the world, and who complained he always found all mirrors untrustworthy, at last discovered his real image reflected in the water. He thus applies his fable: — "Je parle à tous: et cette erreur extrême, Est un mal que chacun se plait d'entretenir, Notre âme, c'est cet homme amoureux de lui même, Tant de miroirs, ce sont les sottises d'autrui. Miroirs, de nos défauts les peintres légitimes, Et quant au canal, c'est celui Qui chacun sait, le livre des MAXIMES."

It is just this: the book is a mirror in which we all see ourselves. This has made it so unpopular. It is too true. We dislike to be told of our faults, while we only like to be told of our neighbour's. Notwithstanding Rousseau's assertion, it is young men, who, before they know their own faults and only know their neighbours', that read and thoroughly appreciate Rochefoucauld.

After so many varied opinions he then pleases us more and seems far truer than he is in reality, it is impossible to give any general conclusion of such distinguished writers on the subject.

Each reader will form his own opinion of the merits of the author and his book. To some, both will seem deserving of the highest praise; to others both will seem deserving of the highest censure. The truest judgment as to the author will be found in the remarks of a countryman of his own, as to the book in the remarks of a countryman of ours.

As to the author, M. Sainte Beuve says:—"C'était un misanthrope poli, insinuant, souriant, qui précédait de bien peu et préparait avec charme l'autre MISANTHROPE."

As to the book, Mr. Hallam says: —"Among the books in ancient and modern times which record the conclusions of observing men on the moral qualities of their fellows, a high place should be reserved for the Maxims of Rochefoucauld."

REFLECTIONS;
OR, SENTENCES AND MORAL MAXIMS

Our virtues are most frequently but vices disguised.

1. —What we term virtue is often but a mass of various actions and divers interests, which fortune, or our own industry, manage to arrange; and it is not always from valour or from chastity that men are brave, and women chaste.

["Who combats bravely is not therefore brave, He dreads a death-bed like the meanest slave; Who reasons wisely is not therefore wise, His pride in reasoning, not in acting, lies."—Pope, Moral Essays, Ep. i. line 115.]

2. —Self-love is the greatest of flatterers.

3. —Whatever discoveries have been made in the region of self-love, there remain many unexplored territories there.

[This is the first hint of the system the author tries to develope. He wishes to find in vice a motive for all our actions, but this does not suffice him; he is obliged to call other passions to the help of his system and to confound pride, vanity, interest and egotism with self love. This confusion destroys the unity of his principle.]

4. —Self love is more cunning than the most cunning man in the world.

5. —The duration of our passions is no more dependant upon us than the duration of our life.
[Then what becomes of free will?]

6. —Passion often renders the most clever man a fool, and even sometimes renders the most foolish man clever.

7. —Great and striking actions which dazzle the eyes are represented by politicians as the effect of great designs, instead of which they are commonly caused by the temper and the passions. Thus the war between Augustus and Anthony, which is set down to the ambition they entertained of making themselves masters of the world, was probably but an effect of jealousy.

8. —The passions are the only advocates which always persuade. They are a natural art, the rules of which are infallible; and the simplest man with passion will be more persuasive than the most eloquent without.
[See Maxim 249 which is an illustration of this.]

9. —The passions possess a certain injustice and self interest

which makes it dangerous to follow them, and in reality we should distrust them even when they appear most trustworthy.

10. —In the human heart there is a perpetual generation of passions; so that the ruin of one is almost always the foundation of another.

11. —Passions often produce their contraries: avarice sometimes leads to prodigality, and prodigality to avarice; we are often obstinate through weakness and daring through timidity.

12. —Whatever care we take to conceal our passions under the appearances of piety and honour, they are always to be seen through these veils.
[The 1st edition, 1665, preserves the image perhaps better—"however we may conceal our passions under the veil, etc., there is always some place where they peep out."]

13. —Our self love endures more impatiently the condemnation of our tastes than of our opinions.

14. —Men are not only prone to forget benefits and injuries; they even hate those who have obliged them, and cease to hate those who have injured them. The necessity of revenging an injury or of recompensing a benefit seems a slavery to which they are unwilling to submit.

15. —The clemency of Princes is often but policy to win the affections of the people.

["So many are the advantages which monarchs gain by clemency, so greatly does it raise their fame and endear them to their subjects, that it is generally happy for them to have an opportunity of displaying it."—Montesquieu, Esprit Des Lois, Lib. VI., C. 21.]

16. —This clemency of which they make a merit, arises oftentimes from vanity, sometimes from idleness, oftentimes from fear, and almost always from all three combined.

[La Rochefoucauld is content to paint the age in which he lived. Here the clemency spoken of is nothing more than an expression of the policy of Anne of Austria. Rochefoucauld had sacrificed all to her; even the favour of Cardinal Richelieu, but when she became regent she bestowed her favours upon those she hated; her friends were forgotten. The reader will hereby see that the age in which the writer lived best interprets his maxims.]

17. —The moderation of those who are happy arises from the calm which good fortune bestows upon their temper.

18. —Moderation is caused by the fear of exciting the envy and contempt which those merit who are intoxicated with their good fortune; it is a vain display of our strength of mind, and in short the moderation of men at their greatest height is only a desire to appear

greater than their fortune.

19. —We have all sufficient strength to support the misfortunes of others.

20. —The constancy of the wise is only the talent of concealing the agitation of their hearts.

[Thus wisdom is only hypocrisy, says a commentator. This definition of constancy is a result of maxim 18.]

21. —Those who are condemned to death affect sometimes a constancy and contempt for death which is only the fear of facing it; so that one may say that this constancy and contempt are to their mind what the bandage is to their eyes.

[See this thought elaborated in maxim 504.]

22. —Philosophy triumphs easily over past evils and future evils; but present evils triumph over it.

23. —Few people know death, we only endure it, usually from determination, and even from stupidity and custom; and most men only die because they know not how to prevent dying.

24. —When great men permit themselves to be cast down by the continuance of misfortune, they show us that they were only sustained by ambition, and not by their mind; so that PLUS a great

vanity, heroes are made like other men.

[Both these maxims have been rewritten and made conciser by the author; the variations are not worth quoting.]

25. —We need greater virtues to sustain good than evil fortune.

["Prosperity doth best discover vice, but adversity do th best discover virtue."—Lord Bacon, Essays, (1625), "Of Adversity".]

26. —Neither the sun nor death can be looked at without winking.

27. —People are often vain of their passions, even of the worst, but envy is a passion so timid and shame-faced that no one ever dare avow her.

28. —Jealousy is in a manner just and reasonable, as it tends to preserve a good which belongs, or which we believe belongs to us, on the other hand envy is a fury which cannot endure the happiness of others.

29. —The evil that we do does not attract to us so much persecution and hatred as our good qualities.

30. —We have more strength than will; and it is often merely for an excuse we say things are impossible.

31. —If we had no faults we should not take so much pleasure in noting those of others.

32. —Jealousy lives upon doubt; and comes to an end or becomes a fury as soon as it passes from doubt to certainty.

33. —Pride indemnifies itself and loses nothing even when it casts away vanity.
[See maxim 450, where the author states, what we take from our other faults we add to our pride.]

34. —If we had no pride we should not complain of that of others.
["The proud are ever most provoked by pride."—Cowper, Conversation 160.]

35. —Pride is much the same in all men, the only difference is the method and manner of showing it.
["Pride bestowed on all a common friend."—Pope, Essay On Man, Ep. ii., line 273.]

36. —It would seem that nature, which has so wisely ordered the organs of our body for our happiness, has also given us pride to spare us the mortification of knowing our imperfections.

37. —Pride has a larger part than goodness in our remonstrances

with those who commit faults, and we reprove them not so much to correct as to persuade them that we ourselves are free from faults.

38. —We promise according to our hopes; we perform according to our fears.

["The reason why the Cardinal (Mazarin) deferred so long to grant the favours he had promised, was because he was persuaded that hope was much more capable of keeping men to their duty than gratitude."—Racine, Fragments Historiques.]

39. —Interest speaks all sorts of tongues and plays all sorts of characters; even that of disinterestedness.

40. —Interest blinds some and makes some see.

41. —Those who apply themselves too closely to little things often become incapable of great things.

42. —We have not enough strength to follow all our reason.

43. —A man often believes himself leader when he is led; as his mind endeavours to reach one goal, his heart insensibly drags him towards another.

44. —Strength and weakness of mind are mis-named; they are really only the good or happy arrangement of our bodily organs.

45. —The caprice of our temper is even more whimsical than that of Fortune.

46. —The attachment or indifference which philosophers have shown to life is only the style of their self love, about which we can no more dispute than of that of the palate or of the choice of colours.

47. —Our temper sets a price upon every gift that we receive from fortune.

48. —Happiness is in the taste, and not in the things themselves; we are happy from possessing what we like, not from possessing what others like.

49. —We are never so happy or so unhappy as we suppose.

50. —Those who think they have merit persuade themselves that they are honoured by being unhappy, in order to persuade others and themselves that they are worthy to be the butt of fortune.

["Ambition has been so strong as to make very miserable men take comfort that they were supreme in misery; and certain it is, that where we cannot distinguish ourselves by something excellent, we begin to take a complacency in some singular infirmities, follies, or defects of one kind or other." —Burke, On The Sublime And Beautiful, (1756), Part I, Sect. XVII.]

51. —Nothing should so much diminish the satisfaction which we feel with ourselves as seeing that we disapprove at one time of that which we approve of at another.

52. —Whatever difference there appears in our fortunes, there is nevertheless a certain compensation of good and evil which renders them equal.

53. —Whatever great advantages nature may give, it is not she alone, but fortune also that makes the hero.

54. —The contempt of riches in philosophers was only a hidden desire to avenge their merit upon the injustice of fortune, by despising the very goods of which fortune had deprived them; it was a secret to guard themselves against the degradation of poverty, it was a back way by which to arrive at that distinction which they could not gain by riches.

["It is always easy as well as agreeable for the inferior ranks of mankind to claim merit from the contempt of that pomp and pleasure which fortune has placed beyond their reach. The virtue of the primitive Christians, like that of the first Romans, was very frequently guarded by poverty and ignorance."—Gibbon, Decline And Fall, Chap. 15.]

55. —The hate of favourites is only a love of favour. The

envy of NOT possessing it, consoles and softens its regrets by the contempt it evinces for those who possess it, and we refuse them our homage, not being able to detract from them what attracts that of the rest of the world.

56. —To establish ourselves in the world we do everything to appear as if we were established.

57. —Although men flatter themselves with their great actions, they are not so often the result of a great design as of chance.

58. —It would seem that our actions have lucky or unlucky stars to which they owe a great part of the blame or praise which is given them.

59. —There are no accidents so unfortunate from which skilful men will not draw some advantage, nor so fortunate that foolish men will not turn them to their hurt.

60. —Fortune turns all things to the advantage of those on whom she smiles.

61. —The happiness or unhappiness of men depends no less upon their dispositions than their fortunes.
["Still to ourselves in every place consigned our own felicity we make or find." —Goldsmith, Traveller, 431.]

62.—Sincerity is an openness of heart; we find it in very few people; what we usually see is only an artful dissimulation to win the confidence of others.

63.—The aversion to lying is often a hidden ambition to render our words credible and weighty, and to attach a religious aspect to our conversation.

64.—Truth does not do as much good in the world, as its counterfeits do evil.

65.—There is no praise we have not lavished upon Prudence; and yet she cannot assure to us the most trifling event.

[The author corrected this maxim several times, in 1665 it is No. 75; 1666, No. 66; 1671-5, No. 65; in the last edition it stands as at present. In the first he quotes Juvenal, Sat. X., line 315. " Nullum numen habes si sit Prudentia, nos te; Nos facimus, Fortuna, deam, coeloque locamus." Applying to Prudence what Juvenal does to Fortune, and with much greater force.]

66.—A clever man ought to so regulate his interests that each will fall in due order. Our greediness so often troubles us, making us run after so many things at the same time, that while we too eagerly look after the least we miss the greatest.

67. —What grace is to the body good sense is to the mind.

68. —It is difficult to define love; all we can say is, that in the soul it is a desire to rule, in the mind it is a sympathy, and in the body it is a hidden and delicate wish to possess what we love—plus many mysteries.

["Love is the love of one singularly, with desire to be singularly beloved."—Hobbes, Leviathan, (1651), Part I, Chapter VI.]

69. —If there is a pure love, exempt from the mixture of our other passions, it is that which is concealed at the bottom of the heart and of which even ourselves are ignorant.

70. —There is no disguise which can long hide love where it exists, nor feign it where it does not.

71. —There are few people who would not be ashamed of being beloved when they love no longer.

72. —If we judge of love by the majority of its results it rather resembles hatred than friendship.

73. —We may find women who have never indulged in an intrigue, but it is rare to find those who have intrigued but once.

["Yet there are some, they say, who have had None; But those who have, ne'er end with only one." —Lord Byron, Don Juan, Canto iii., stanza 4.]

74. —There is only one sort of love, but there are a thousand different copies.

75. —Neither love nor fire can subsist without perpetual motion; both cease to live so soon as they cease to hope, or to fear.
[So Lord Byron {Stanzas, (1819), stanza 3} says of Love— "Like chiefs of faction, His life is action."]

76. —There is real love just as there are real ghosts; every person speaks of it, few persons have seen it.
["Oh Love! no habitant of earth thou art— An unseen seraph, we believe in thee— A faith whose martyrs are the broken heart,— But never yet hath seen, nor e'er shall see The naked eye, thy form as it should be." —Lord Byron, Childe Harold, Canto iv., stanza 121.]

77. —Love lends its name to an infinite number of engagements (Commerces) which are attributed to it, but with which it has no more concern than the Doge has with all that is done in Venice.

78. —The love of justice is simply in the majority of men the fear of suffering injustice.

79. —Silence is the best resolve for him who distrusts himself.

80. —What renders us so changeable in our friendship is, that it is difficult to know the qualities of the soul, but easy to know those of the mind.

81. —We can love nothing but what agrees with us, and we can only follow our taste or our pleasure when we prefer our friends to ourselves; nevertheless it is only by that preference that friendship can be true and perfect.

82. —Reconciliation with our enemies is but a desire to better our condition, a weariness of war, the fear of some unlucky accident.

["Thus terminated that famous war of the Fronde. The Duke de la Rochefoucauld desired peace because of his dangerous wounds and ruined castles, which had made him dread even worse events. On the other side the Queen, who had shown herself so ungrateful to her too ambitious friends, did not cease to feel the bitterness of their resentment. 'I wish,' said she, 'it were always night, because daylight shows me so many who have betrayed me.'"—Memoires De Madame De Motteville, Tom. IV., p. 60.

Another proof that although these maxims are in some cases of universal application, they were based entirely on the experience of the age in which the author lived.]

83. —What men term friendship is merely a partnership with a collection of reciprocal interests, and an exchange of favours—in

fact it is but a trade in which self love always expects to gain something.

84. —It is more disgraceful to distrust than to be deceived by our friends.

85. —We often persuade ourselves to love people who are more powerful than we are, yet interest alone produces our friendship; we do not give our hearts away for the good we wish to do, but for that we expect to receive.

86. —Our distrust of another justifies his deceit.

87. —Men would not live long in society were they not the dupes of each other.

88. —Self love increases or diminishes for us the good qualities of our friends, in proportion to the satisfaction we feel with them, and we judge of their merit by the manner in which they act towards us.

89. —Everyone blames his memory, no one blames his judgment.

90. —In the intercourse of life, we please more by our faults than by our good qualities.

91. —The largest ambition has the least appearance of ambition when it meets with an absolute impossibility in compassing its object.

92. —To awaken a man who is deceived as to his own merit is to do him as bad a turn as that done to the Athenian madman who was happy in believing that all the ships touching at the port belonged to him.

93. —Old men delight in giving good advice as a consolation for the fact that they can no longer set bad examples.

94. —Great names degrade instead of elevating those who know not how to sustain them.

95. —The test of extraordinary merit is to see those who envy it the most yet obliged to praise it.

96. —A man is perhaps ungrateful, but often less chargeable with ingratitude than his benefactor is.

97. —We are deceived if we think that mind and judgment are two different matters: judgment is but the extent of the light of the mind. This light penetrates to the bottom of matters; it remarks all that can be remarked, and perceives what appears imperceptible.

Therefore we must agree that it is the extent of the light in the mind that produces all the effects which we attribute to judgment.

98. —Everyone praises his heart, none dare praise their understanding.

99. —Politeness of mind consists in thinking chaste and refined thoughts.

100. —Gallantry of mind is saying the most empty things in an agreeable manner.

101. —Ideas often flash across our minds more complete than we could make them after much labour.

102. —The head is ever the dupe of the heart.

103. —Those who know their minds do not necessarily know their hearts.

104. —Men and things have each their proper perspective; to judge rightly of some it is necessary to see them near, of others we can never judge rightly but at a distance.

105. —A man for whom accident discovers sense, is not a rational being. A man only is so who understands, who distinguishes,

who tests it.

106. —To understand matters rightly we should understand their details, and as that knowledge is almost infinite, our knowledge is always superficial and imperfect.

107. —One kind of flirtation is to boast we never flirt.

108. —The head cannot long play the part of the heart.

109. —Youth changes its tastes by the warmth of its blood, age retains its tastes by habit.

110. —Nothing is given so profusely as advice.

111. —The more we love a woman the more prone we are to hate her.

112. —The blemishes of the mind, like those of the face, increase by age.

113. —There may be good but there are no pleasant marriages.

114. —We are inconsolable at being deceived by our enemies and betrayed by our friends, yet still we are often content to be thus served by ourselves.

115. —It is as easy unwittingly to deceive oneself as to deceive others.

116. —Nothing is less sincere than the way of asking and giving advice. The person asking seems to pay deference to the opinion of his friend, while thinking in reality of making his friend approve his opinion and be responsible for his conduct. The person giving the advice returns the confidence placed in him by eager and disinterested zeal, in doing which he is usually guided only by his own interest or reputation.

["I have often thought how ill-natured a maxim it was which on many occasions I have heard from people of good understanding, 'That as to what related to private conduct no one was ever the better for advice.' But upon further examination I have resolved with myself that the maxim might be admitted without any violent prejudice to mankind. For in the manner advice was generally given there was no reason I thought to wonder it should be so ill received, something there was which strangely inverted the case, and made the giver to be the only gainer. For by what I could observe in many occurrences of our lives, that which we called giving advice was properly taking an occasion to show our own wisdom at another's expense. On the other side to be instructed or to receive advice on the terms usually prescribed to us was little better than tamely to afford another the occasion of raising himself a character from our defects."—Lord Shaftesbury, Characteristics, i., 153.]

117. —The most subtle of our acts is to simulate blindness for snares that we know are set for us. We are never so easily deceived as when trying to deceive.

118. —The intention of never deceiving often exposes us to deception.

119. —We become so accustomed to disguise ourselves to others that at last we are disguised to ourselves.
["Those who quit their proper character, to assume what does not belong to them, are, for the greater part, ignorant both of the character they leave, and of the character they assume."—Burke, Reflections On The Revolution In France, (1790), Paragraph 19.]

120. —We often act treacherously more from weakness than from a fixed motive.

121. —We frequently do good to enable us with impunity to do evil.

122. —If we conquer our passions it is more from their weakness than from our strength.

123. —If we never flattered ourselves we should have but scant pleasure.

124. —The most deceitful persons spend their lives in blaming deceit, so as to use it on some great occasion to promote some great interest.

125. —The daily employment of cunning marks a little mind, it generally happens that those who resort to it in one respect to protect themselves lay themselves open to attack in another.
["With that low cunning which in fools supplies, And amply, too, the place of being wise." —Churchill, Rosciad, 117.]

126. —Cunning and treachery are the offspring of incapacity.

127. —The true way to be deceived is to think oneself more knowing than others.

128. —Too great cleverness is but deceptive delicacy, true delicacy is the most substantial cleverness.

129. —It is sometimes necessary to play the fool to avoid being deceived by cunning men.

130. —Weakness is the only fault which cannot be cured.

131. —The smallest fault of women who give themselves up to love is to love.

132. —It is far easier to be wise for others than to be so for oneself.

[Hence the proverb, "A man who is his own lawyer has a fool for his client."]

133. —The only good examples are those, that make us see the absurdity of bad originals.

134. —We are never so ridiculous from the habits we have as from those that we affect to have.

135. —We sometimes differ more widely from ourselves than we do from others.

136. —There are some who never would have loved if they never had heard it spoken of.

137. —When not prompted by vanity we say little.

138. —A man would rather say evil of himself than say nothing.

["Montaigne's vanity led him to talk perpetually of himself, and as often happens to vain men, he would rather talk of his own failings than of any foreign subject."— Hallam, Literature Of Europe.]

139. —One of the reasons that we find so few persons rational and agreeable in conversation is there is hardly a person who does not think more of what he wants to say than of his answer to what is said. The most clever and polite are content with only seeming attentive while we perceive in their mind and eyes that at the very time they are wandering from what is said and desire to return to what they want to say. Instead of considering that the worst way to persuade or please others is to try thus strongly to please ourselves, and that to listen well and to answer well are some of the greatest charms we can have in conversation.

["An absent man can make but few observations, he can pursue nothing steadily because his absences make him lose his way. They are very disagreeable and hardly to be tolerated in old age, but in youth they cannot be forgiven." —Lord Chesterfield, Letter 195.]

140. —If it was not for the company of fools, a witty man would often be greatly at a loss.

141. —We often boast that we are never bored, but yet we are so conceited that we do not perceive how often we bore others.

142. —As it is the mark of great minds to say many things in a few words, so it is that of little minds to use many words to say nothing.

["So much they talked, so very little said." —Churchill,

Rosciad, 550.

"Men who are unequal to the labour of discussing an argument or wish to avoid it, are willing enough to suppose that much has been proved because much has been said." —Junius, Jan. 1769.]

143. —It is oftener by the estimation of our own feelings that we exaggerate the good qualities of others than by their merit, and when we praise them we wish to attract their praise.

144. —We do not like to praise, and we never praise without a motive. Praise is flattery, artful, hidden, delicate, which gratifies differently him who praises and him who is praised. The one takes it as the reward of merit, the other bestows it to show his impartiality and knowledge.

145. —We often select envenomed praise which, by a reaction upon those we praise, shows faults we could not have shown by other means.

146. —Usually we only praise to be praised.

147. —Few are sufficiently wise to prefer censure which is useful to praise which is treacherous.

148. —Some reproaches praise; some praises reproach.
["Damn with faint praise, assent with civil leer, and, without

sneering, teach the rest to sneer." —Pope, Essay On Man, (1733), Epistle To Dr. Arbuthnot.]

149. —The refusal of praise is only the wish to be praised twice.

[The modesty which pretends to refuse praise is but in truth a desire to be praised more highly. Edition 1665.]

150. —The desire which urges us to deserve praise strengthens our good qualities, and praise given to wit, valour, and beauty, tends to increase them.

151. —It is easier to govern others than to prevent being governed.

152. —If we never flattered ourselves the flattery of others would not hurt us.

153. —Nature makes merit but fortune sets it to work.

154. —Fortune cures us of many faults that reason could not.

155. —There are some persons who only disgust with their abilities, there are persons who please even with their faults.

156. —There are persons whose only merit consists in saying

and doing stupid things at the right time, and who ruin all if they change their manners.

157. —The fame of great men ought always to be estimated by the means used to acquire it.

158. —Flattery is base coin to which only our vanity gives currency.

159. —It is not enough to have great qualities, we should also have the management of them.

160. —However brilliant an action it should not be esteemed great unless the result of a great motive.

161. —A certain harmony should be kept between actions and ideas if we desire to estimate the effects that they produce.

162. —The art of using moderate abilities to advantage wins praise, and often acquires more reputation than real brilliancy.

163. —Numberless arts appear foolish whose secret motives are most wise and weighty.

164. —It is much easier to seem fitted for posts we do not fill than for those we do.

165. —Ability wins us the esteem of the true men, luck that of the people.

166. —The world oftener rewards the appearance of merit than merit itself.

167. —Avarice is more opposed to economy than to liberality.

168. —However deceitful hope may be, yet she carries us on pleasantly to the end of life.
["Hope travels through, nor quits us when we die." —Pope, Essay On Man, Ep. ii.]

169. —Idleness and fear keeps us in the path of duty, but our virtue often gets the praise.

170. —If one acts rightly and honestly, it is difficult to decide whether it is the effect of integrity or skill.

171. —As rivers are lost in the sea so are virtues in self.

172. —If we thoroughly consider the varied effects of indifference we find we miscarry more in our duties than in our interests.

173. —There are different kinds of curiosity: one springs from interest, which makes us desire to know everything that may be profitable to us; another from pride, which springs from a desire of knowing what others are ignorant of.

174. —It is far better to accustom our mind to bear the ills we have than to speculate on those which may befall us.
["Rather bear those ills we have Than fly to others that we know not of." —Shakespeare, Hamlet, Act III, Scene I, Hamlet.]

175. —Constancy in love is a perpetual inconstancy which causes our heart to attach itself to all the qualities of the person we love in succession, sometimes giving the preference to one, sometimes to another. This constancy is merely inconstancy fixed, and limited to the same person.

176. —There are two kinds of constancy in love, one arising from incessantly finding in the loved one fresh objects to love, the other from regarding it as a point of honour to be constant.

177. —Perseverance is not deserving of blame or praise, as it is merely the continuance of tastes and feelings which we can neither create or destroy.

178. —What makes us like new studies is not so much the weariness we have of the old or the wish for change as the desire to

be admired by those who know more than ourselves, and the hope of advantage over those who know less.

179. —We sometimes complain of the levity of our friends to justify our own by anticipation.

180. —Our repentance is not so much sorrow for the ill we have done as fear of the ill that may happen to us.

181. —One sort of inconstancy springs from levity or weakness of mind, and makes us accept everyone's opinion, and another more excusable comes from a surfeit of matter.

182. —Vices enter into the composition of virtues as poison into that of medicines. Prudence collects and blends the two and renders them useful against the ills of life.

183. —For the credit of virtue we must admit that the greatest misfortunes of men are those into which they fall through their crimes.

184. —We admit our faults to repair by our sincerity the evil we have done in the opinion of others.
[In the edition of 1665 this maxim stands as No. 200. "We never admit our faults except through vanity."]

185. —There are both heroes of evil and heroes of good.

186. —We do not despise all who have vices, but we do despise all who have not virtues.

["If individuals have no virtues their vices may be of use to us."—Junius, 5th Oct. 1771.]

187. —The name of virtue is as useful to our interest as that of vice.

188. —The health of the mind is not less uncertain than that of the body, and when passions seem furthest removed we are no less in danger of infection than of falling ill when we are well.

189. —It seems that nature has at man's birth fixed the bounds of his virtues and vices.

190. —Great men should not have great faults.

191. —We may say vices wait on us in the course of our life as the landlords with whom we successively lodge, and if we travelled the road twice over I doubt if our experience would make us avoid them.

192. —When our vices leave us we flatter ourselves with the idea we have left them.

193. —There are relapses in the diseases of the mind as in those of the body; what we call a cure is often no more than an intermission or change of disease.

194. —The defects of the mind are like the wounds of the body. Whatever care we take to heal them the scars ever remain, and there is always danger of their reopening.

195. —The reason which often prevents us abandoning a single vice is having so many.

196. —We easily forget those faults which are known only to ourselves.

[Seneca says "Innocentem quisque se dicit respiciens testem non conscientiam."]

197. —There are men of whom we can never believe evil without having seen it. Yet there are very few in whom we should be surprised to see it.

198. —We exaggerate the glory of some men to detract from that of others, and we should praise Prince Condé and Marshal Turenne much less if we did not want to blame them both.

[The allusion to Condé and Turenne gives the date at which these maxims were published in 1665. Condé and Turenne were after their campaign with the Imperialists at the height of their fame. It proves the truth of the remark of Tacitus, "Populus neminem sine aemulo sinit."— Tac. Ann. xiv.]

199. —The desire to appear clever often prevents our being so.

200. —Virtue would not go far did not vanity escort her.

201. —He who thinks he has the power to content the world greatly deceives himself, but he who thinks that the world cannot be content with him deceives himself yet more.

202. —Falsely honest men are those who disguise their faults both to themselves and others; truly honest men are those who know them perfectly and confess them.

203. —He is really wise who is nettled at nothing.

204. —The coldness of women is a balance and burden they add to their beauty.

205. —Virtue in woman is often the love of reputation and repose.

206. —He is a truly good man who desires always to bear the inspection of good men.

207. —Folly follows us at all stages of life. If one appears wise 'tis but because his folly is proportioned to his age and fortune.

208. —There are foolish people who know and who skilfully use their folly.

209. —Who lives without folly is not so wise as he thinks.

210. —In growing old we become more foolish—and more wise.

211. —There are people who are like farces, which are praised but for a time (however foolish and distasteful they may be).
[The last clause is added from Edition of 1665.]

212. —Most people judge men only by success or by fortune.

213. —Love of glory, fear of shame, greed of fortune, the desire to make life agreeable and comfortable, and the wish to depreciate others are often causes of that bravery so vaunted among men.
[Junius said of the Marquis of Granby, "He was as brave as a total absence of all feeling and reflection could make him."—21st Jan. 1769.]

214. —Valour in common soldiers is a perilous method of

earning their living.

["Men venture necks to gain a fortune, The soldier does it ev'ry day, (Eight to the week) for sixpence pay." —Samuel Butler, Hudibras, Part II., canto i., line 512.]

215. —Perfect bravery and sheer cowardice are two extremes rarely found. The space between them is vast, and embraces all other sorts of courage. The difference between them is not less than between faces and tempers. Men will freely expose themselves at the beginning of an action, and relax and be easily discouraged if it should last. Some are content to satisfy worldly honour, and beyond that will do little else. Some are not always equally masters of their timidity. Others allow themselves to be overcome by panic; others charge because they dare not remain at their posts. Some may be found whose courage is strengthened by small perils, which prepare them to face greater dangers. Some will dare a sword cut and flinch from a bullet; others dread bullets little and fear to fight with swords. These varied kinds of courage agree in this, that night, by increasing fear and concealing gallant or cowardly actions, allows men to spare themselves. There is even a more general discretion to be observed, for we meet with no man who does all he would have done if he were assured of getting off scot-free; so that it is certain that the fear of death does somewhat subtract from valour.

216. —Perfect valour is to do without witnesses what one would do before all the world.

["It is said of untrue valours that some men's valours are in the eyes of them that look on."—Bacon, Advancement Of Learning, (1605), Book I, Section II, paragraph 5.]

217. —Intrepidity is an extraordinary strength of soul which raises it above the troubles, disorders, and emotions which the sight of great perils can arouse in it: by this strength heroes maintain a calm aspect and preserve their reason and liberty in the most surprising and terrible accidents.

218. —Hypocrisy is the homage vice pays to virtue.

[So Massillon, in one of his sermons, "Vice pays homage to virtue in doing honour to her appearance."

So Junius, writing to the Duke of Grafton, says, "You have done as much mischief to the community as Machiavel, if Machiavel had not known that an appearance of morals and religion are useful in society."—28 Sept. 1771.]

219. —Most men expose themselves in battle enough to save their honor, few wish to do so more than sufficiently, or than is necessary to make the design for which they expose themselves succeed.

220. —Vanity, shame, and above all disposition, often make men brave and women chaste.

["Vanity bids all her sons be brave and all her daughters chaste and courteous. But why do we need her instruction?"—Sterne, Sermons.]

221. —We do not wish to lose life; we do wish to gain glory, and this makes brave men show more tact and address in avoiding death, than rogues show in preserving their fortunes.

222. —Few persons on the first approach of age do not show wherein their body, or their mind, is beginning to fail.

223. —Gratitude is as the good faith of merchants: it holds commerce together; and we do not pay because it is just to pay debts, but because we shall thereby more easily find people who will lend.

224. —All those who pay the debts of gratitude cannot thereby flatter themselves that they are grateful.

225. —What makes false reckoning, as regards gratitude, is that the pride of the giver and the receiver cannot agree as to the value of the benefit.
["The first foundation of friendship is not the power of conferring benefits, but the equality with which they are received, and may be returned."—Junius's Letter To The King.]

226. —Too great a hurry to discharge of an obligation is a kind

of ingratitude.

227. —Lucky people are bad hands at correcting their faults; they always believe that they are right when fortune backs up their vice or folly.

["The power of fortune is confessed only by the miserable, for the happy impute all their success to prudence and merit."—Swift, Thoughts On Various Subjects]

228. —Pride will not owe, self-love will not pay.

229. —The good we have received from a man should make us excuse the wrong he does us.

230. —Nothing is so infectious as example, and we never do great good or evil without producing the like. We imitate good actions by emulation, and bad ones by the evil of our nature, which shame imprisons until example liberates.

231. —It is great folly to wish only to be wise.

232. —Whatever pretext we give to our afflictions it is always interest or vanity that causes them.

233. —In afflictions there are various kinds of hypocrisy. In one, under the pretext of weeping for one dear to us we bemoan

ourselves; we regret her good opinion of us, we deplore the loss of our comfort, our pleasure, our consideration. Thus the dead have the credit of tears shed for the living. I affirm 'tis a kind of hypocrisy which in these afflictions deceives itself. There is another kind not so innocent because it imposes on all the world, that is the grief of those who aspire to the glory of a noble and immortal sorrow. After Time, which absorbs all, has obliterated what sorrow they had, they still obstinately obtrude their tears, their sighs their groans, they wear a solemn face, and try to persuade others by all their acts, that their grief will end only with their life. This sad and distressing vanity is commonly found in ambitious women. As their sex closes to them all paths to glory, they strive to render themselves celebrated by showing an inconsolable affliction. There is yet another kind of tears arising from but small sources, which flow easily and cease as easily. One weeps to achieve a reputation for tenderness, weeps to be pitied, weeps to be bewept, in fact one weeps to avoid the disgrace of not weeping!

["In grief the Pleasure is still uppermost; and the affliction we suffer has no resemblance to absolute pain which is always odious, and which we endeavour to shake off as soon as possible."—Burke, Sublime And Beautiful, (1756), Part I, Sect. V.]

234. —It is more often from pride than from ignorance that we are so obstinately opposed to current opinions; we find the first places taken, and we do not want to be the last.

235. —We are easily consoled at the misfortunes of our friends when they enable us to prove our tenderness for them.

236. —It would seem that even self-love may be the dupe of goodness and forget itself when we work for others. And yet it is but taking the shortest way to arrive at its aim, taking usury under the pretext of giving, in fact winning everybody in a subtle and delicate manner.

237. —No one should be praised for his goodness if he has not strength enough to be wicked. All other goodness is but too often an idleness or powerlessness of will.

238. —It is not so dangerous to do wrong to most men, as to do them too much good.

239. —Nothing flatters our pride so much as the confidence of the great, because we regard it as the result of our worth, without remembering that generally 'tis but vanity, or the inability to keep a secret.

240. —We may say of conformity as distinguished from beauty, that it is a symmetry which knows no rules, and a secret harmony of features both one with each other and with the colour and appearance of the person.

241. —Flirtation is at the bottom of woman's nature, although all do not practise it, some being restrained by fear, others by sense.

["By nature woman is a flirt, but her flirting changes both in the mode and object according to her opinions." — Rousseau, Emile.]

242. —We often bore others when we think we cannot possibly bore them.

243. —Few things are impossible in themselves; application to make them succeed fails us more often than the means.

244. —Sovereign ability consists in knowing the value of things.

245. —There is great ability in knowing how to conceal one's ability.

["You have accomplished a great stroke in diplomacy when you have made others think that you have only very average abilities." —La Bruyère.]

246. —What seems generosity is often disguised ambition, that despises small to run after greater interest.

247. —The fidelity of most men is merely an invention of self-love to win confidence; a method to place us above others and to render us depositaries of the most important matters.

248. —Magnanimity despises all, to win all.

249. —There is no less eloquence in the voice, in the eyes and in the air of a speaker than in his choice of words.

250. —True eloquence consists in saying all that should be, not all that could be said.

251. —There are people whose faults become them, others whose very virtues disgrace them.
["There are faults which do him honour, and virtues that disgrace him." —Junius, Letter Of 28th May, 1770.]

252. —It is as common to change one's tastes, as it is uncommon to change one's inclinations.

253. —Interest sets at work all sorts of virtues and vices.

254. —Humility is often a feigned submission which we employ to supplant others. It is one of the devices of Pride to lower us to raise us; and truly pride transforms itself in a thousand ways, and is never so well disguised and more able to deceive than when it hides itself under the form of humility.
["Grave and plausible enough to be thought fit for business." —Junius, Letter To The Duke Of Grafton.

"He saw a cottage with a double coach-house, A cottage of gentility, And the devil was pleased, for his darling sin Is the pride that apes humility." —Southey, Devil's Walk.]

255. —All feelings have their peculiar tone of voice, gestures and looks, and this harmony, as it is good or bad, pleasant or unpleasant, makes people agreeable or disagreeable.

256. —In all professions we affect a part and an appearance to seem what we wish to be. Thus the world is merely composed of actors.

["All the world's a stage, and all the men and women merely players."—Shakespeare, As You Like It, Act II, Scene VII, Jaques.

"Life is no more than a dramatic scene, in which the hero should preserve his consistency to the last."—Junius.]

257. —Gravity is a mysterious carriage of the body invented to conceal the want of mind.

["Gravity is the very essence of imposture."—Shaftesbury, Characteristics, p. 11, vol. I.

"The very essence of gravity is design, and consequently deceit; a taught trick to gain credit with the world for more sense and knowledge than a man was worth, and that with all its pretensions it was no better, but often worse, than what a French wit had long ago defined it—a mysterious carriage of the body to cover the defects of the mind."—Sterne, Tristram Shandy, vol. I., chap. ii.]

258. —Good taste arises more from judgment than wit.

259. —The pleasure of love is in loving, we are happier in the passion we feel than in that we inspire.

260. —Civility is but a desire to receive civility, and to be esteemed polite.

261. —The usual education of young people is to inspire them with a second self-love.

262. —There is no passion wherein self-love reigns so powerfully as in love, and one is always more ready to sacrifice the peace of the loved one than his own.

263. —What we call liberality is often but the vanity of giving, which we like more than that we give away.

264. —Pity is often a reflection of our own evils in the ills of others. It is a delicate foresight of the troubles into which we may fall. We help others that on like occasions we may be helped ourselves, and these services which we render, are in reality benefits we confer on ourselves by anticipation.

["Grief for the calamity of another is pity, and ariseth from the imagination that a like calamity may befal himself; and therefore is called compassion." —Hobbes, Leviathan, (1651), Part I, Chapter VI.]

265. —A narrow mind begets obstinacy, and we do not easily believe what we cannot see.

["Stiff in opinion, always in the wrong." —Dryden, Absalom And Achitophel, line 547.]

266. —We deceive ourselves if we believe that there are violent passions like ambition and love that can triumph over others. Idleness, languishing as she is, does not often fail in being mistress; she usurps authority over all the plans and actions of life; imperceptibly consuming and destroying both passions and virtues.

267. —A quickness in believing evil without having sufficiently examined it, is the effect of pride and laziness. We wish to find the guilty, and we do not wish to trouble ourselves in examining the crime.

268. —We credit judges with the meanest motives, and yet we desire our reputation and fame should depend upon the judgment of men, who are all, either from their jealousy or pre-occupation or want of intelligence, opposed to us—and yet 'tis only to make these men decide in our favour that we peril in so many ways both our peace and our life.

269. —No man is clever enough to know all the evil he does.

270. —One honour won is a surety for more.

271. —Youth is a continual intoxication; it is the fever of reason.
["The best of life is but intoxication."—Lord Byron, Don Juan, Canto II, stanza 179.
In the 1st Edition, 1665, the maxim finishes with— "it is the fever of health, the folly of reason."]

272. —Nothing should so humiliate men who have deserved great praise, as the care they have taken to acquire it by the smallest means.

273. —There are persons of whom the world approves who have no merit beyond the vices they use in the affairs of life.

274. —The beauty of novelty is to love as the flower to the fruit; it lends a lustre which is easily lost, but which never returns.

275. —Natural goodness, which boasts of being so apparent, is often smothered by the least interest.

276. —Absence extinguishes small passions and increases great ones, as the wind will blow out a candle, and blow in a fire.

277. —Women often think they love when they do not love. The business of a love affair, the emotion of mind that sentiment induces, the natural bias towards the pleasure of being loved, the difficulty of refusing, persuades them that they have real passion when they have but flirtation.

["And if in fact she takes a Grande Passion, It is a very serious thing indeed: Nine times in ten 'tis but caprice or fashion, Coquetry, or a wish to take the lead, The pride of a mere child with a new sash on. Or wish to make a rival's bosom bleed: But the Tenth instance will be a tornado, For there's no saying what they will or may do." —Lord Byron, Don Juan, canto xii. stanza 77.]

278. —What makes us so often discontented with those who transact business for us is that they almost always abandon the interest of their friends for the interest of the business, because they wish to have the honour of succeeding in that which they have undertaken.

279. —When we exaggerate the tenderness of our friends towards us, it is often less from gratitude than from a desire to exhibit our own merit.

280. —The praise we give to new comers into the world arises from the envy we bear to those who are established.

281. —Pride, which inspires, often serves to moderate envy.

282. —Some disguised lies so resemble truth, that we should judge badly were we not deceived.

283. —Sometimes there is not less ability in knowing how to use than in giving good advice.

284. —There are wicked people who would be much less dangerous if they were wholly without goodness.

285. —Magnanimity is sufficiently defined by its name, nevertheless one can say it is the good sense of pride, the most noble way of receiving praise.

286. —It is impossible to love a second time those whom we have really ceased to love.

287. —Fertility of mind does not furnish us with so many resources on the same matter, as the lack of intelligence makes us hesitate at each thing our imagination presents, and hinders us from at first discerning which is the best.

288. —There are matters and maladies which at certain times remedies only serve to make worse; true skill consists in knowing when it is dangerous to use them.

289. —Affected simplicity is refined imposture.

290. —There are as many errors of temper as of mind.

291. —Man's merit, like the crops, has its season.

292. —One may say of temper as of many buildings; it has divers aspects, some agreeable, others disagreeable.

293. —Moderation cannot claim the merit of opposing and overcoming Ambition: they are never found together. Moderation is the languor and sloth of the soul, Ambition its activity and heat.

294. —We always like those who admire us, we do not always like those whom we admire.

295. —It is well that we know not all our wishes.

296. —It is difficult to love those we do not esteem, but it is no less so to love those whom we esteem much more than ourselves.

297. —Bodily temperaments have a common course and rule which imperceptibly affect our will. They advance in combination, and successively exercise a secret empire over us, so that, without our perceiving it, they become a great part of all our actions.

298. —The gratitude of most men is but a secret desire of receiving greater benefits.

[Hence the common proverb "Gratitude is merely a lively sense of favors to come."]

299. —Almost all the world takes pleasure in paying small debts; many people show gratitude for trifling, but there is hardly one who does not show ingratitude for great favours.

300. —There are follies as catching as infections.

301. —Many people despise, but few know how to bestow wealth.

302. —Only in things of small value we usually are bold enough not to trust to appearances.

303. —Whatever good quality may be imputed to us, we ourselves find nothing new in it.

304. —We may forgive those who bore us, we cannot forgive those whom we bore.

305. —Interest which is accused of all our misdeeds often should be praised for our good deeds.

306. —We find very few ungrateful people when we are able to confer favours.

307. —It is as proper to be boastful alone as it is ridiculous to be so in company.

308. —Moderation is made a virtue to limit the ambition of the great; to console ordinary people for their small fortune and equally small ability.

309. —There are persons fated to be fools, who commit follies not only by choice, but who are forced by fortune to do so.

310. —Sometimes there are accidents in our life the skilful extrication from which demands a little folly.

311. —If there be men whose folly has never appeared, it is because it has never been closely looked for.

312. —Lovers are never tired of each other,—they always speak of themselves.

313. —How is it that our memory is good enough to retain the least triviality that happens to us, and yet not good enough to recollect how often we have told it to the same person?

["Old men who yet retain the memory of things past, and forget how often they have told them, are most tedious companions." —Montaigne, Essays, Book I, Chapter IX.]

314. —The extreme delight we take in talking of ourselves should warn us that it is not shared by those who listen.

315. —What commonly hinders us from showing the recesses of our heart to our friends, is not the distrust we have of them, but that we have of ourselves.

316. —Weak persons cannot be sincere.

317. —'Tis a small misfortune to oblige an ungrateful man; but it is unbearable to be obliged by a scoundrel.

318. —We may find means to cure a fool of his folly, but there are none to set straight a cross-grained spirit.

319. —If we take the liberty to dwell on their faults we cannot long preserve the feelings we should hold towards our friends and benefactors.

320. —To praise princes for virtues they do not possess is but to reproach them with impunity.

["Praise undeserved is satire in disguise," quoted by Pope from a poem which has not survived, "The Garland," by Mr. Broadhurst. "In some cases exaggerated or inappropriate praise becomes the most severe satire."— Scott, Woodstock.]

321. —We are nearer loving those who hate us, than those who love us more than we desire.

322. —Those only are despicable who fear to be despised.

323. —Our wisdom is no less at the mercy of Fortune than our goods.

324. —There is more self-love than love in jealousy.

325. —We often comfort ourselves by the weakness of evils, for which reason has not the strength to console us.

326. —Ridicule dishonours more than dishonour itself.
["No," says a commentator, "Ridicule may do harm, but it cannot dishonour; it is vice which confers dishonour."]

327. —We own to small faults to persuade others that we have not great ones.

328. —Envy is more irreconcilable than hatred.

329. —We believe, sometimes, that we hate flattery —we only dislike the method.

["But when I tell him he hates flatterers, He says he does, being then most flattered." —Shakespeare, Julius Caesar, Act II, Scene I, Decius.]

330. —We pardon in the degree that we love.

331. —It is more difficult to be faithful to a mistress when one is happy, than when we are ill-treated by her.

332. —Women do not know all their powers of flirtation.

333. —Women cannot be completely severe unless they hate.

334. —Women can less easily resign flirtations than love.

335. —In love deceit almost always goes further than mistrust.

336. —There is a kind of love, the excess of which forbids jealousy.

337. —There are certain good qualities as there are senses, and those who want them can neither perceive nor understand them.

338. —When our hatred is too bitter it places us below those

whom we hate.

339. —We only appreciate our good or evil in proportion to our self-love.

340. —The wit of most women rather strengthens their folly than their reason.
["Women have an entertaining tattle, and sometimes wit, but for solid reasoning and good sense I never knew one in my life that had it, and who reasoned and acted consequentially for four and twenty hours together."—Lord Chesterfield, Letter 129.]

341. —The heat of youth is not more opposed to safety than the coldness of age.

342. —The accent of our native country dwells in the heart and mind as well as on the tongue.

343. —To be a great man one should know how to profit by every phase of fortune.

344. —Most men, like plants, possess hidden qualities which chance discovers.

345. —Opportunity makes us known to others, but more to ourselves.

346. —If a woman's temper is beyond control there can be no control of the mind or heart.

347. —We hardly find any persons of good sense, save those who agree with us.
["That was excellently observed, say I, when I read an author when his opinion agrees with mine."—Swift, Thoughts On Various Subjects.]

348. —When one loves one doubts even what one most believes.

349. —The greatest miracle of love is to eradicate flirtation.

350. —Why we hate with so much bitterness those who deceive us is because they think themselves more clever than we are.
["I could pardon all his (Louis XI.'s) deceit, but I cannot forgive his supposing me capable of the gross folly of being duped by his professions."—Sir Walter Scott, Quentin Durward.]

351. —We have much trouble to break with one, when we no longer are in love.

352. —We almost always are bored with persons with whom we should not be bored.

353. —A gentleman may love like a lunatic, but not like a beast.

354. —There are certain defects which well mounted glitter like virtue itself.

355. —Sometimes we lose friends for whose loss our regret is greater than our grief, and others for whom our grief is greater than our regret.

356. —Usually we only praise heartily those who admire us.

357. —Little minds are too much wounded by little things; great minds see all and are not even hurt.

358. —Humility is the true proof of Christian virtues; without it we retain all our faults, and they are only covered by pride to hide them from others, and often from ourselves.

359. —Infidelities should extinguish love, and we ought not to be jealous when we have cause to be so. No persons escape causing jealousy who are worthy of exciting it.

360. —We are more humiliated by the least infidelity towards us, than by our greatest towards others.

361. —Jealousy is always born with love, but does not always die with it.

362. —Most women do not grieve so much for the death of their lovers for love's sake, as to show they were worthy of being beloved.

363. —The evils we do to others give us less pain than those we do to ourselves.

364. —We well know that it is bad taste to talk of our wives; but we do not so well know that it is the same to speak of ourselves.

365. —There are virtues which degenerate into vices when they arise from Nature, and others which when acquired are never perfect. For example, reason must teach us to manage our estate and our confidence, while Nature should have given us goodness and valour.

366. —However we distrust the sincerity of those whom we talk with, we always believe them more sincere with us than with others.

367. —There are few virtuous women who are not tired of their part.

["Every woman is at heart a rake."—Pope, Moral Essays, ii.]

368. —The greater number of good women are like concealed treasures, safe as no one has searched for them.

369. —The violences we put upon ourselves to escape love are often more cruel than the cruelty of those we love.

370. —There are not many cowards who know the whole of their fear.

371. —It is generally the fault of the loved one not to perceive when love ceases.

372. —Most young people think they are natural when they are only boorish and rude.

373. —Some tears after having deceived others deceive ourselves.

374. —If we think we love a woman for love of herself we are greatly deceived.

375. —Ordinary men commonly condemn what is beyond them.

376. —Envy is destroyed by true friendship, flirtation by true love.

377. —The greatest mistake of penetration is not to have fallen short, but to have gone too far.

378. —We may bestow advice, but we cannot inspire the conduct.

379. —As our merit declines so also does our taste.

380. —Fortune makes visible our virtues or our vices, as light does objects.

381. —The struggle we undergo to remain faithful to one we love is little better than infidelity.

382. —Our actions are like the rhymed ends of blank verses (Bouts-Rimés) where to each one puts what construction he pleases.

[The Bouts-Rimés was a literary game popular in the 17th and 18th centuries—the rhymed words at the end of a line being given for others to fill up. Thus Horace Walpole being given, "brook, why, crook, I," returned the burlesque verse— "I sits with my toes in a Brook, And if any one axes me Why? I gies 'em a rap with my Crook, 'Tis constancy makes me, ses I."]

383. —The desire of talking about ourselves, and of putting our faults in the light we wish them to be seen, forms a great part of our sincerity.

384. —We should only be astonished at still being able to be astonished.

385. —It is equally as difficult to be contented when one has too much or too little love.

386. —No people are more often wrong than those who will not allow themselves to be wrong.

387. —A fool has not stuff in him to be good.

388. —If vanity does not overthrow all virtues, at least she makes them totter.

389. —What makes the vanity of others unsupportable is that it wounds our own.

390. —We give up more easily our interest than our taste.

391. —Fortune appears so blind to none as to those to whom she has done no good.

392. —We should manage fortune like our health, enjoy it when it is good, be patient when it is bad, and never resort to strong remedies but in an extremity.

393. —Awkwardness sometimes disappears in the camp, never in the court.

394. —A man is often more clever than one other, but not than all others.

395. —We are often less unhappy at being deceived by one we loved, than on being deceived.

396. —We keep our first lover for a long time—if we do not get a second.

397. —We have not the courage to say generally that we have no faults, and that our enemies have no good qualities; but in fact we are not far from believing so.

398. —Of all our faults that which we most readily admit is idleness: we believe that it makes all virtues ineffectual, and that without utterly destroying, it at least suspends their operation.

399. —There is a kind of greatness which does not depend upon fortune: it is a certain manner what distinguishes us, and which

seems to destine us for great things; it is the value we insensibly set upon ourselves; it is by this quality that we gain the deference of other men, and it is this which commonly raises us more above them, than birth, rank, or even merit itself.

400. —There may be talent without position, but there is no position without some kind of talent.

401. —Rank is to merit what dress is to a pretty woman.

402. —What we find the least of in flirtation is love.

403. —Fortune sometimes uses our faults to exalt us, and there are tiresome people whose deserts would be ill rewarded if we did not desire to purchase their absence.

404. —It appears that nature has hid at the bottom of our hearts talents and abilities unknown to us. It is only the passions that have the power of bringing them to light, and sometimes give us views more true and more perfect than art could possibly do.

405. —We reach quite inexperienced the different stages of life, and often, in spite of the number of our years, we lack experience.
["To most men experience is like the stern lights of a ship which illumine only the track it has passed."— Coleridge.]

406. —Flirts make it a point of honour to be jealous of their lovers, to conceal their envy of other women.

407. —It may well be that those who have trapped us by their tricks do not seem to us so foolish as we seem to ourselves when trapped by the tricks of others.

408. —The most dangerous folly of old persons who have been loveable is to forget that they are no longer so.

["Every woman who is not absolutely ugly thinks herself handsome. The suspicion of age no woman, let her be ever so old, forgives."—Lord Chesterfield, Letter 129.]

409. —We should often be ashamed of our very best actions if the world only saw the motives which caused them.

410. —The greatest effort of friendship is not to show our faults to a friend, but to show him his own.

411. —We have few faults which are not far more excusable than the means we adopt to hide them.

412. —Whatever disgrace we may have deserved, it is almost always in our power to re-establish our character.

["This is hardly a period at which the most irregular character may not be redeemed. The mistakes of one sin find a retreat in patriotism, those of the other in devotion." —Junius, Letter To The King.]

413. —A man cannot please long who has only one kind of wit.

[According to Segrais this maxim was a hit at Racine and Boileau, who, despising ordinary conversation, talked incessantly of literature; but there is some doubt as to Segrais' statement. —Aimé Martin.]

414. —Idiots and lunatics see only their own wit.

415. —Wit sometimes enables us to act rudely with impunity.

416. —The vivacity which increases in old age is not far removed from folly.

["How ill white hairs become a fool and jester."— Shakespeare, King Henry IV, Part II, Act. V, Scene V, King.

"Can age itself forget that you are now in the last act of life? Can grey hairs make folly venerable, and is there no period to be reserved for meditation or retirement."— Junius, To The Duke Of Bedford, 19th Sept. 1769.]

417. —In love the quickest is always the best cure.

418. —Young women who do not want to appear flirts, and old men who do not want to appear ridiculous, should not talk of love as

a matter wherein they can have any interest.

419. —We may seem great in a post beneath our capacity, but we oftener seem little in a post above it.

420. —We often believe we have constancy in misfortune when we have nothing but debasement, and we suffer misfortunes without regarding them as cowards who let themselves be killed from fear of defending themselves.

421. —Conceit causes more conversation than wit.

422. —All passions make us commit some faults, love alone makes us ridiculous.
["In love we all are fools alike."—Gay, The Beggar's Opera, (1728), Act III, Scene I, Lucy.]

423. —Few know how to be old.

424. —We often credit ourselves with vices the reverse of what we have, thus when weak we boast of our obstinacy.

425. —Penetration has a spice of divination in it which tickles our vanity more than any other quality of the mind.

426. —The charm of novelty and old custom, however opposite

to each other, equally blind us to the faults of our friends.

["Two things the most opposite blind us equally, custom and novelty." —La Bruyère, Des Judgements.]

427. —Most friends sicken us of friendship, most devotees of devotion.

428. —We easily forgive in our friends those faults we do not perceive.

429. —Women who love, pardon more readily great indiscretions than little infidelities.

430. —In the old age of love as in life we still survive for the evils, though no longer for the pleasures.

["The youth of friendship is better than its old age." —Hazlitt's Characteristics, 229.]

431. —Nothing prevents our being unaffected so much as our desire to seem so.

432. —To praise good actions heartily is in some measure to take part in them.

433. —The most certain sign of being born with great qualities is to be born without envy.

434. —When our friends have deceived us we owe them but indifference to the tokens of their friendship, yet for their misfortunes we always owe them pity.

435. —Luck and temper rule the world.

436. —It is far easier to know men than to know man.

437. —We should not judge of a man's merit by his great abilities, but by the use he makes of them.

438. —There is a certain lively gratitude which not only releases us from benefits received, but which also, by making a return to our friends as payment, renders them indebted to us.
["And understood not that a grateful mind, By owing owes not, but is at once Indebted and discharged." —Milton, Paradise Lost.]

439. —We should earnestly desire but few things if we clearly knew what we desired.

440. —The cause why the majority of women are so little given to friendship is, that it is insipid after having felt love.
["Those who have experienced a great passion neglect friendship, and those who have united themselves to friendship have nought to do with love." —La Bruyère, Du Coeur.]

441. —As in friendship so in love, we are often happier from ignorance than from knowledge.

442. —We try to make a virtue of vices we are loth to correct.

443. —The most violent passions give some respite, but vanity always disturbs us.

444. —Old fools are more foolish than young fools.
["Malvolio. Infirmity, that decays the wise, doth ever make the better fool. Clown. God send you, sir, a speedy infirmity, for the better increasing of your folly." —Shakespeare, Twelfth Night, Act I, Scene V.]

445. —Weakness is more hostile to virtue than vice.

446. —What makes the grief of shame and jealousy so acute is that vanity cannot aid us in enduring them.

447. —Propriety is the least of all laws, but the most obeyed.
[Honour has its supreme laws, to which education is bound to conform....Those things which honour forbids are more rigorously forbidden when the laws do not concur in the prohibition, and those it commands are more strongly insisted upon when they happen not to be commanded by law. —Montesquieu, The Spirit

Of Laws, b. 4, c. ii.]

448. —A well-trained mind has less difficulty in submitting to than in guiding an ill-trained mind.

449. —When fortune surprises us by giving us some great office without having gradually led us to expect it, or without having raised our hopes, it is well nigh impossible to occupy it well, and to appear worthy to fill it.

450. —Our pride is often increased by what we retrench from our other faults.
["The loss of sensual pleasures was supplied and compensated by spiritual pride." —Gibbon, Decline And Fall, chap. xv.]

451. —No fools so wearisome as those who have some wit.

452. —No one believes that in every respect he is behind the man he considers the ablest in the world.

453. —In great matters we should not try so much to create oppo-rtunities as to utilise those that offer themselves.
[Yet Lord Bacon says "A wise man will make more opportunities than he finds." —Essays, (1625), "Of Ceremonies and Respects"]

454. —There are few occasions when we should make a bad bargain by giving up the good on condition that no ill was said of us.

455. —However disposed the world may be to judge wrongly, it far oftener favours false merit than does justice to true.

456. —Sometimes we meet a fool with wit, never one with discretion.

457. —We should gain more by letting the world see what we are than by trying to seem what we are not.

458. —Our enemies come nearer the truth in the opinions they form of us than we do in our opinion of ourselves.

459. —There are many remedies to cure love, yet none are infallible.

460. —It would be well for us if we knew all our passions make us do.

461. —Age is a tyrant who forbids at the penalty of life all the pleasures of youth.

462. —The same pride which makes us blame faults from which we believe ourselves free causes us to despise the good

qualities we have not.

463. —There is often more pride than goodness in our grief for our enemies' miseries; it is to show how superior we are to them, that we bestow on them the sign of our compassion.

464. —There exists an excess of good and evil which surpasses our comprehension.

465. —Innocence is most fortunate if it finds the same protection as crime.

466. —Of all the violent passions the one that becomes a woman best is love.

467. —Vanity makes us sin more against our taste than reason.

468. —Some bad qualities form great talents.

469. —We never desire earnestly what we desire in reason.

470. —All our qualities are uncertain and doubtful, both the good as well as the bad, and nearly all are creatures of opportunities.

471. —In their first passion women love their lovers, in all the others they love love.

["In her first passion woman loves her lover, In all her others what she loves is love." —Lord Byron, Don Juan, Canto iii., stanza 3.

"We truly love once, the first time; the subsequent passions are more or less involuntary." —La Bruyère, Du Coeur.]

472. —Pride as the other passions has its follies. We are ashamed to own we are jealous, and yet we plume ourselves in having been and being able to be so.

473. —However rare true love is, true friendship is rarer.

["It is more common to see perfect love than real friendship." —La Bruyère, Du Coeur.]

474. —There are few women whose charm survives their beauty.

475. —The desire to be pitied or to be admired often forms the greater part of our confidence.

476. —Our envy always lasts longer than the happiness of those we envy.

477. —The same firmness that enables us to resist love enables us to make our resistance durable and lasting. So weak persons who are always excited by passions are seldom really possessed of any.

478. —Fancy does not enable us to invent so many different contradictions as there are by nature in every heart.

479. —It is only people who possess firmness who can possess true gentleness. In those who appear gentle it is generally only weakness, which is readily converted into harshness.

480. —Timidity is a fault which is dangerous to blame in those we desire to cure of it.

481. —Nothing is rarer than true good nature, those who think they have it are generally only pliant or weak.

482. —The mind attaches itself by idleness and habit to whatever is easy or pleasant. This habit always places bounds to our knowledge, and no one has ever yet taken the pains to enlarge and expand his mind to the full extent of its capacities.

483. —Usually we are more satirical from vanity than malice.

484. —When the heart is still disturbed by the relics of a passion it is proner to take up a new one than when wholly cured.

485. —Those who have had great passions often find all their lives made miserable in being cured of them.

486. —More persons exist without self-love than without envy.

["I do not believe that there is a human creature in his senses arrived at maturity, that at some time or other has not been carried away by this passion (envy) in good earnest, and yet I never met with any who dared own he was guilty of it, but in jest." —Mandeville, Fable Of The Bees; Remark N.]

487. —We have more idleness in the mind than in the body.

488. —The calm or disturbance of our mind does not depend so much on what we regard as the more important things of life, as in a judicious or injudicious arrangement of the little things of daily occurrence.

489. —However wicked men may be, they do not dare openly to appear the enemies of virtue, and when they desire to persecute her they either pretend to believe her false or attribute crimes to her.

490. —We often go from love to ambition, but we never return from ambition to love.

["Men commence by love, finish by ambition, and do not find a quieter seat while they remain there."—La Bruyère, Du Coeur.]

491. —Extreme avarice is nearly always mistaken, there is no passion which is oftener further away from its mark, nor upon which the present has so much power to the prejudice of the future.

492. —Avarice often produces opposite results: there are an infinite number of persons who sacrifice their property to doubtful and distant expectations, others mistake great future advantages for small present interests.

[Aimé Martin says, "The author here confuses greediness, the desire and avarice—passions which probably have a common origin, but produce different results. The greedy man is nearly always desirous to possess, and often foregoes great future advantages for small present interests. The avaricious man, on the other hand, mistakes present advantages for the great expectations of the future. Both desire to possess and enjoy. But the miser possesses and enjoys nothing but the pleasure of possessing; he risks nothing, gives nothing, hopes nothing, his life is centred in his strong box, beyond that he has no want."]

493. —It appears that men do not find they have enough faults, as they increase the number by certain peculiar qualities that they affect to assume, and which they cultivate with so great assiduity that at length they become natural faults, which they can no longer correct.

494. —What makes us see that men know their faults better than we imagine, is that they are never wrong when they speak of their conduct; the same self-love that usually blinds them enlightens them, and gives them such true views as to make them suppress or

disguise the smallest thing that might be censured.

495. —Young men entering life should be either shy or bold; a solemn and sedate manner usually degenerates into impertinence.

496. —Quarrels would not last long if the fault was only on one side.

497. —It is valueless to a woman to be young unless pretty, or to be pretty unless young.

498. —Some persons are so frivolous and fickle that they are as far removed from real defects as from substantial qualities.

499. —We do not usually reckon a woman's first flirtation until she has had a second.

500. —Some people are so self-occupied that when in love they find a mode by which to be engrossed with the passion without being so with the person they love.

501. —Love, though so very agreeable, pleases more by its ways than by itself.

502. —A little wit with good sense bores less in the long run than much wit with ill nature.

503. —Jealousy is the worst of all evils, yet the one that is least pitied by those who cause it.

504. —Thus having treated of the hollowness of so many apparent virtues, it is but just to say something on the hollowness of the contempt for death. I allude to that contempt of death which the heathen boasted they derived from their unaided understanding, without the hope of a future state. There is a difference between meeting death with courage and despising it. The first is common enough, the last I think always feigned. Yet everything that could be has been written to persuade us that death is no evil, and the weakest of men, equally with the bravest, have given many noble examples on which to found such an opinion, still I do not think that any man of good sense has ever yet believed in it. And the pains we take to persuade others as well as ourselves amply show that the task is far from easy. For many reasons we may be disgusted with life, but for none may we despise it. Not even those who commit suicide regard it as a light matter, and are as much alarmed and startled as the rest of the world if death meets them in a different way than the one they have selected. The difference we observe in the courage of so great a number of brave men, is from meeting death in a way different from what they imagined, when it shows itself nearer at one time than at another. Thus it ultimately happens that having despised death when they were ignorant of it, they dread it when they become acquainted with it. If we could avoid seeing it with all its surroundings, we

might perhaps believe that it was not the greatest of evils. The wisest and bravest are those who take the best means to avoid reflecting on it, as every man who sees it in its real light regards it as dreadful. The necessity of dying created all the constancy of philosophers. They thought it but right to go with a good grace when they could not avoid going, and being unable to prolong their lives indefinitely, nothing remained but to build an immortal reputation, and to save from the general wreck all that could be saved. To put a good face upon it, let it suffice, not to say all that we think to ourselves, but rely more on our nature than on our fallible reason, which might make us think we could approach death with indifference. The glory of dying with courage, the hope of being regretted, the desire to leave behind us a good reputation, the assurance of being enfranchised from the miseries of life and being no longer dependent on the wiles of fortune, are resources which should not be passed over. But we must not regard them as infallible. They should affect us in the same proportion as a single shelter affects those who in war storm a fortress. At a distance they think it may afford cover, but when near they find it only a feeble protection. It is only deceiving ourselves to imagine that death, when near, will seem the same as at a distance, or that our feelings, which are merely weaknesses, are naturally so strong that they will not suffer in an attack of the rudest of trials. It is equally as absurd to try the effect of self-esteem and to think it will enable us to count as naught what will of necessity destroy it. And the mind in which we trust to find so many resources will be far too weak in the struggle to persuade us in the way we wish. For it is this which betrays us so frequently, and which, instead of filling us with contempt of death, serves but to show us all that is frightful and fearful. The most it can do for us is to persuade us to avert our gaze and fix it on other objects. Cato and Brutus each selected noble ones. A lackey sometime ago contented himself by dancing on the scaffold when he was about to be broken on the wheel. So however diverse the motives they but realize the same result. For the rest it is a fact that whatever difference there may be between the peer and the peasant, we have constantly seen both the one and the other meet death with the same composure. Still there is always this difference, that the contempt the peer shows for death is but the love of fame which hides death from his sight; in the peasant it is but the result of his limited vision that hides from him the extent of the evil, end leaves him free to reflect on other things.